Church

Church

Amy Welborn

Our Sunday Visitor Publishing Division
Our Sunday Visitor, Inc.
Huntington, Indiana 46750

Nihil Obstat
Rev. Michael Heintz
Censor Librorum

Imprimatur
✠ John M. D'Arcy
Bishop of Fort Wayne-South Bend
June 12, 2001

The *Nihil Obstat* and *Imprimatur* are official declarations that a book or pamphlet is free of doctrinal or moral error. No implication is contained therein that those who have granted the *Nihil Obstat* or *Imprimatur* agree with the contents, opinions, or statements expressed.

Scripture excerpts unless otherwise indicated are taken from the *New American Bible with Revised New Testament,* copyright © 1986, 1970 by the Confraternity of Christian Doctrine, Washington, D.C. Used with permission. All rights reserved. No part of the *New American Bible* may be reproduced by any means without permission in writing from the copyright owner. Excerpts from the English translation of the *Catechism of the Catholic Church, Second Edition,* for use in the United States of America, copyright © 1994 and 1997, United States Catholic Conference — Libreria Editrice Vaticana. Used with permission. Every reasonable effort has been made to determine copyright holders. If any copyrighted materials have been inadvertently used without proper credit being given in one manner or another, please notify Our Sunday Visitor in writing so that future editions may be corrected accordingly.

Our Sunday Visitor Publishing Division
Our Sunday Visitor, Inc.
200 Noll Plaza
Huntington, IN 46750

ISBN: 978-0-87973-981-2 (Inventory No. 981)
LCCCN: 2001-131191

Cover design by Tyler Ottinger
Cover photo by John Zierten
Interior design by Sherri L. Hoffman
Interior illustrations by James Douglas Adams

PRINTED IN THE UNITED STATES OF AMERICA

For Christopher

CONTENTS

ONE

"What Church Do You Go To?"

It happened on the first day of eighth grade.

There I was, in a new school in a new town in a completely new part of the country, just trying to figure out my thirteen-year-old life: where I was supposed to go next, what bus I was supposed to take home, and exactly what was and wasn't cool down here in this strange land called Tennessee.

Sitting in a rickety portable classroom, getting ready for a history class, I was startled by a voice in my ear.

"My name's Donna," she said, in a sweet Southern drawl. "What's yours?"

I told her. Next question?

"What church do you go to?"

I said the word: *Catholic*.

She meditated deeply on this for a second, then nodded knowingly.

"I thought so," she announced. "You look like a Catholic. I'm Baptist."

I looked like a Catholic. Okay. And what is so Catholic, exactly, about short brown hair, glasses, and braces? So I guess that means freckles and a mop of long red hair is the look all the Baptist girls were after in 1973?

No, I didn't say that. In fact, I didn't say anything, because before I could regroup my brain, the bell rang, and Tennessee history class — the story of a lot of Baptists, Methodists, and Presbyterians, but not too many Catholics — began.

But that wasn't the end, either of our friendship or that particular conversation. As her second question to me made perfectly clear, Donna was very, very interested in religion, knew more about the Bible than almost any adult I'd ever encountered, and had lots and lots of questions about this Catholic identity that apparently glinted right off my wire-rimmed glasses for anyone to see.

"Why do y'all worship Mary?"

"Why do you think the pope can't be wrong about anything?"

"Why do your churches have statues when the Bible says not to have graven images?"

"Why do you call your priests 'Father' when the Bible says not to?"

I had never, ever, thought about even one of those questions before. I'd taken every bit of my faith for granted, never asked why, never wondered, never even tried to figure out what was different about being Catholic and why — until Donna asked me. And asked and asked. The girl just would not and could not give up. She forced me to think, and to be honest, she shamed me — shamed me into facing some cold, hard truths about myself.

Here I was, a cradle Catholic who never missed Mass and even said the Rosary once in a while (okay, mostly to help me go to sleep at night, but still . . .), and I couldn't answer even one simple question about the unique aspects of this faith I said I believed. What kind of a Catholic was I?

On top of that, she knew so much about her own faith! She was my age, but she could quote Scripture passages that I'd never heard of. As I learned when I went over to visit her, she read two chapters of the Bible every night — and even having company didn't stop her. Why didn't I take my faith as seriously as she was taking hers? What was my excuse?

So, that year, I stopped making excuses. It's sort of a bizarre picture, but I have to reveal that it really did happen this way. During study hall, I'd sit in the library of my big public junior high school, those huge green volumes of the *New Catholic Encyclopedia* open in front of me, racing through articles on "Assumption" or "Papal Infallibility" or "Infant Baptism," hoping that at least enough of the important stuff would sink in, and I could explain it to Donna.

I don't know how successful I was. Probably not very. I'm sure that Donna is still a very happy Baptist today, still reading Scripture every night, and teaching her own children to do the very same thing. Maybe she learned a little bit about Catholicism. Knowing what I was able to tell her, if it was anything, it was indeed a very little bit.

How about you?

Have you ever been challenged the way Donna challenged me?

If so, perhaps the challenge came from friends at school, like mine did. Maybe you've found a little pamphlet in a public restroom or on a park bench that asks you, in big bold letters, "ARE YOU SAVED?" And you have to wonder, *Am I?*

Evangelists might have appeared at your door. Perhaps you've even encountered these kinds of questions and challenges from right in your own family. A surprising number of members of fundamentalist churches were actually cradle Catholics, and they have children, grandchildren, nieces, and nephews they would be very happy to bring along on the trip.

You can be sure, though, that if your Catholic faith hasn't been challenged by a fundamentalist Christian yet, it will be. It will happen at school or work. It will happen in your neighborhood. And there's no doubt it will happen if you go to college. Believe it or not, there really are groups whose specific ministry is all about convincing Catholic college students that their Catholic faith is not only wrong, but also dangerous to their eternal salvation.

Are you ready?

If you're not, fasten your seat belts. You need to get ready, and let me tell you why before we head out on this bumpy ride to the land of Truth, Wisdom, and a Whole Lotta Big Words.

You simply must understand that when fundamentalists start peppering you with questions, their motive isn't simple curiosity. Sowing doubt is what it's really all about.

We have to be honest about this. Many, many fundamentalist Christians believe that the Catholic Church leads its followers nowhere but to hell. Not all of them buy this, of course. Later on in this chapter, we'll briefly run through the diversity you'll find among those who call themselves "fundamentalist" and "evangelical."

But a startling number of them believe that you're doomed. There are actually entire "ministries" devoted to "saving Catholics." Most fundamentalist churches send missionaries to traditionally Catholic countries in Latin America and Europe. Why? To bring Jesus Christ to the poor, ignorant souls who inhabit those lands — implying, of course, that the Catholic Church has been silent on that minor matter.

Those kinds of groups, "evangelization" movements, and anti-Catholic books and pamphlets don't come out of a respect for the ancient Catholic faith. Nope, they're rooted in nothing less than a deep conviction that the Catholic faith leads people away from God, and that it's the fundamentalist's mission to put them back on the right path.

And believe it or not, despite all of this, your hard-core evangelizing fundamentalist will deny, deny, deny that she's anti-Catholic.

"But we love Catholics!" she'll proclaim. "That's why we want to bring them to Jesus!"

Thanks a bunch. Somehow, I don't think we're defining our terms exactly the same way. So, this is how the whole deal usually ends up working:

You'll field a question or two about your faith — those same questions I was asked when I was thirteen. Some you can sort of answer. Some leave you stumped, silent, and squirming.

And without even saying a direct word about it, your friend has planted a seed of doubt.

As a matter of fact, I don't know why my Church does these things, you think. *What else about it don't I know?*

Next, they might start showing you passages in the Bible that seem to contradict the teachings of the Catholic faith.

But, you wonder, *how can that be? Our faith is supposed to come from the Bible, isn't it?*

Finally, they'll ask that all-important, life-defining question. "Are you saved? If you were to die tonight, would you go to heaven? Are you sure?"

You consider your baptism, your prayers, your participation in Mass and the other sacraments, your volunteer work — all those things, your Catholic faith has taught you, that bring you closer to God.

But the barrage of questions — the seeds of doubt — have begun to sprout:

My friend seems to know so much more about religion than I do. Maybe she knows more about this salvation stuff. Plus, she's telling me that a lot of this Catholic stuff isn't in the Bible, and she seems to be right. Maybe. . . .

How could I be Catholic my whole life and still be so unsure about things? Why isn't what I hear in church as clear as what my friend is telling me?

Maybe she knows something I don't. Maybe she has an answer that I don't have. I wonder what it is?

And there you go, off into the wild blue yonder, away from the Catholic faith.

But we're not going to let that happen, right? Right. And let me tell you why.

Because you, my friend, are very, very interested in truth.

You're not about to accept arguments that are based on fear, half-truths, or manipulations of Bible passages taken out of context.

You're not about to just sit and believe what someone outside the Catholic faith tells you about that same faith.

You're smarter than that.

You know in your heart that the Catholic faith *does* bring you to Christ. In fact, the Catholic Church *is* the Body of Christ on earth, established by Jesus himself, living, teaching, loving, and healing today, the same way Jesus did when He walked the earth.

You know because of all this — because the Church belongs to Christ, teaches Christ, preaches Christ, and *is* Christ in the world, and because eternal salvation comes through Christ — that *of course* you can find salvation through the Catholic Church!

It just makes sense.

Be real. The Church has been around for two thousand years. Lots of people have dealt with these issues before, and have done so very successfully. Believe it or not, there are quite a few former fundamentalists who, once they started investigating what the Catholic Church was really all about, rather than blindly accepting what they were taught by their own pastors and churches, found themselves so convinced by what they found that they became Catholic themselves! Check out "For a Deeper Look" at the end of this book for the titles of some books these folks have written about their journeys.

So don't worry. If you have a Donna or two in your life, don't run the other way when she plops down behind you in class. Don't see her as a walking, talking acne infestation, good for nothing but a big dose of Stridex.

Maybe, just maybe, you could see her as a blessing, sent by Someone (gee — who could that be?) to finally, at long last, get you thinking about this thing we call "faith."

EQUIPMENT YOU'LL NEED

Here's a list of stuff that will come in handy in your conversations with fundamentalist Christians:

❑ A Catholic Bible with good study notes: the New American Bible and the Jerusalem Bible are two excellent, reliable versions.

❑ A copy of the *Catechism of the Catholic Church*. This is an absolute must. Your friend is going to try to tell you "what the Catholic Church teaches" pretty much constantly. Having the *Catechism* around for handy reference is a good way to show her how incorrect her perceptions are.

❑ A commitment to regular Bible reading and study of your faith.

❑ A good attitude:

     ✓ Loving
     ✓ Patient
     ✓ Respectful
     ✓ Confident in the truth

Who Are They?

So who are these people, these fundamentalists bubbling with questions and promising salvation?

And do they all have red hair and freckles?

Okay, okay. Let's lay down our first rule: No stereotypes.

You've probably spent enough time watching TV to have a firm grasp of the rather mindless stereotypes the media use to describe human beings: Southerners are slow-witted, Italians are all packing it for the mob, and teenagers — well, teenagers are all ignorant, sex-crazed, multipierced slackers, right?

And, of course, we have the fundamentalists: big-haired women and men with Southern accents racing around the planet with a Bible in one hand and a bomb in the other, ready to fling it at the next abortion clinic they happen to pass.

Life is more complex than that, isn't it?

This book is all about finding and sharing the truth. So, just as we're intent on correcting fundamentalist misperceptions of Catholicism, we must, from the very beginning, set aside any shallow stereotypes of fundamentalist Christians we may harbor ourselves.

So let's try to get a little background.

It's not easy to define fundamentalists.

It's not easy to even figure out what to call them. Some people will — indeed proudly — call themselves "fundamentalists," and others would rather be known as "evangelicals." Both terms refer to movements or sets of ideas within Christianity, not any particular denomination.

Let's start with "evangelical." Evangelical Christians, no matter what denomination, share a faith that's rooted in Scripture, the individual experience of finding salvation in Christ, and the conviction of the importance of sharing that faith with the whole world.

(The word *evangelical* comes from the Greek word *euangelion*, which simply means "good news" or, in old English, *god-spell* or, as we say it now, Gospel. That's why we call the writers of the Gospels the "Evangelists." That's why the act of spreading the Good News about Jesus is called "evangelizing.")

Fundamentalist Christians are evangelical, to be sure, but they are a special kind of evangelical Christian: they emphasize taking the Bible literally, and they tend to believe that the more separated Christians are from the world, the better off they are.

The tricky part, then, is while all fundamentalists are evangelicals, not all evangelicals are fundamentalists, by any stretch of the imagination.

We have the same difficulty with terms like "born-again" or "Bible-believing" Christians. Not all you meet who talk about their experiences of being saved or who enjoy a certain style of informal, freewheeling worship are fundamentalists. As a matter of fact, in the course of your life you'll probably meet fellow Catholics who share those kinds of experiences, but there's no way they could ever be called "fundamentalist Christians."

So there's the first complication.

The second is that there's no single "fundamentalist denomination." You'll even find that some Christian denominations have both fundamentalist and non-fundamentalist wings to them.

For example, take Presbyterians. Many Presbyterians are quite liberal in their beliefs, particularly those who belong to what's called the Presbyterian Church (USA). But on the other hand, those who belong to the Orthodox Presbyterian Church or Covenant Presbyterian Churches tend to share quite a few fundamentalist views, and think those liberal Presbyterians are in just as much trouble as any other run-of-the-mill unbeliever. Maybe more.

So that's the way it is within denominations. You probably know that's true from your experience as a Catholic. You might have family members who live and worship on completely opposite sides of the spectrum. Your Uncle Clement will only attend Mass if it's in Latin and thinks it's a horror that you, an actual real-live girl, were an altar server. But then there's your grandmother, who thinks it's a worse horror that women aren't ordained priests and wouldn't hesitate to tell the pope so herself if she had the chance.

Both are Catholics, and both are part of the same Church — though barely, it may seem, at that annual terror called Thanksgiving dinner. But they're still hanging on together nonetheless.

You can't tell a fundamentalist by appearances, either. Some fundamentalists do indeed share really strict views on issues like the length of a woman's hair (see 1 Corinthians

11:6 to understand why), but some don't care. Some fundamentalists wouldn't worship in anything less than a three-
piece suit, and others are just fine with you if you're a guy in
jeans with an earring or two and a ponytail.

So you can't discover who's a fundamentalist by how
they look (now that's a good general life lesson, isn't it?) or
even by what denomination they're a part of. In order to
understand what any fundamentalist Christian is all about,
you have to go further than appearances and labels. You
might even have to do something terrifying and new: actually listen to what they have to say!

What Do They Believe?

Well, now your friend, acquaintance, or accidental lunch
companion has started talking and you've discerned that
something's up. You're hearing a lot of Bible passages quoted
(impressively, from memory), you've been asked if you're
saved, and to be sure, you've been asked obviously skeptical questions about that pope guy. Good clues, there. But
what do they mean?

Let's start with the basic beliefs most fundamentalist
Christians share:

- **"The Bible alone is the source of faith."**
  Fundamentalists believe that God put everything He
  wants us to know about Him in the Bible. That's it.
  Every bit of Christian faith, every teaching, and the
  basis for every practice has to be found in the Bible.

- **"The Bible is the inerrant Word of God."**
  Another apparently obvious idea: There are no mis-
  takes in the Bible, and no real (as opposed to appar-

ent) contradictions. It's God's Word, God is Truth, so of course there are no *untruths* in the Bible of *any* kind. That's what saying the Bible is "inerrant" means.

- **"The Bible must be read according to its plain, literal meaning."**
  The Word of God means what it says. Period. Sure, the fundamentalist will admit that there is symbolic language in the Bible — God is not literally a rock, of course. But beyond those obvious poetic uses of human language, the fundamentalist claims, no interpretation is allowed or necessary.

- **"It's faith alone that saves you."**
  This, along with the "Bible-only" teaching, is really the big one for fundamentalists. We'll go into more detail on it in a later chapter, but the basic meaning of it is this: Human sinfulness is so great that there is not a single thing we can do to save ourselves. By His death on the cross, Jesus paid the price for all of humanity's sin. The only way a person can be saved from the hell that person deserves is by an act of faith in the power of Jesus' death on the cross and everything that means. That's what being "saved" or "born again" is all about: It's a single act, a moment in time, when you turn to Christ and acknowledge Him as your Savior from sin and hell.

  And that's it. A good life has absolutely nothing to do with salvation, according to the fundamentalist. They call those good deeds, prayers, and other virtuous acts "works." And while "works" are certainly fine ways to spend your time, they offer about as much help in getting your soul saved as would pouring over *Leaves of Grass* in preparation for your trigonometry test. Too bad, so sad.

Given this teaching, and given the fact that Catholics believe something just a teeny bit different, the odds are good that at some point you'll have the pleasure of discovering that your fundamentalist friend believes that Catholics aren't saved – from hell. And we're talking to you, buddy.

So . . . What's the Difference?

I know, I know. You're wondering, you're chomping at the bit, you just have to know: What do Catholics believe about all this? Is it really all that different?

Don't we believe that our faith is rooted in Scripture, which we also believe is the Word of God? Don't we believe that salvation lies in faith in Jesus, and that we are indeed saved because of Him?

Well, see, here's the thing.

Words are funny things. Two people can use the exact same words and attach wholly different meanings to them. It's sort of like when your parents declare to you that they're not picky, that they just want you to be "responsible."

Now, to you, there is nothing at all irresponsible about staying out until two in the morning. You got home safely, didn't you? And sure, you had to stay up for thirty-six straight hours to get your "History of the Leaf Blower" paper done, but you got it finished, didn't you? How can anyone say that you're not "responsible?"

Somehow, every time, your parents will find a way, won't they?

What we have here, it seems, is a failure to define words in exactly the same way. It happens all the time in discussions of religion, which is one reason why those very same conversations have a tendency to spin round and round in frustrating, never-ending circles.

So you're hearing "Everything in the Christian faith should be *in* the Bible," and you're thinking, *Sure. Sounds good.*

But what does "in" mean?

Does it mean "explicitly stated in exact terms?" Does it mean "alluded to in some form?" Or does it mean "implied and definitely not contradicting"?

Ah yes, definitions. Kind of important, aren't they?

So, yes, Catholics believe that the Bible is the Word of God, the foundation of our faith. Catholics believe that faith in Christ saves us. Yes to all of that.

But when you start going behind the words, you'll find that our definitions of all of those terms differ from the fundamentalist Christian's definition. So, in order to talk profitably about this, in order to explain and do your own bit of evangelizing, you have to understand those definitions. Otherwise, you'll find yourself swept away, and quickly too, by waves of words that you thought you understood but which the fundamentalist will try to convince you that you don't, and in the process hint to you that Catholicism is something less — *a lot* less — than true Christianity.

But we're not going to let that happen, so let's get rolling.

(Get off the floor, you maniac! I mean *rolling* as in *proceed*, as in *get started*, as in *go to the next chapter*. Do you really have to take me so *literally* all the time?)

THE PERSON YOU'RE TALKING TO

A fundamentalist Christian is a person who believes that:

❏ The Bible should always be interpreted in its literal sense.
❏ The Bible is the only source for Christian beliefs and practices.
❏ Salvation comes in a single act of faith in the power of Jesus' death on the cross.
❏ Human actions have nothing to do with a person's salvation. It's all about that moment of being "saved."

INTERLUDE

Our imaginary discussions with fundamentalist Christians are going to center around two major areas: the Bible and the nature of faith.

We're starting with the Bible for one simple reason: Because *they* do.

Fundamentalist Christians believe that since the Bible should be the only source of faith for a Christian, every argument for a Christian belief must have a Bible verse as its defense — and if a church is preaching and teaching stuff that's "not in the Bible," it has no right to call itself Christian.

(And in case you haven't figured this out, that means *you*. Ms. and Mr. Catholic-not-a-Christian!)

You'll find, incidentally, that while your fundamentalist friend is probably very strong in his knowledge of the Bible, he's considerably weaker in his understanding of Christian history. Let's see if you can compensate for that weakness, okay?

So that's what they'll throw at you: verse after verse from the Bible, telling you why what they believe is right and what you believe is not only wrong, but toxic to your soul.

And you just might start thinking, *Hey, he quoted me a verse saying that we should call no man "father." Can anyone here show me a verse saying that it's okay? No? Then why do we do it? How can we be doing something that the Bible says we shouldn't do? Gee, what else are we doing wrong?*

Whoops! You've made a big mistake. You've swallowed their assumptions like a lovely big bite of chocolate cake, without thinking, without considering the consequences.

Why in the world did you do that?

Why did you just assume that their frame of reference was the right one, the only one, the true one?

Because, you know, it's not.

TWO

"Why Isn't Your Church a 'Bible-Only' Church?"

So there you are, contemplating this big, long list you've been handed by your fundamentalist Christian friend. It's so long, we can't possibly include all of it, but here's how it starts out:

Pope
Purgatory
"Father" Whoever
Immaculate Conception
Rosary
Statues

Oh, did I not tell you the title of this particular list? Sorry, I forgot. This list is very poetically called "Stuff That Catholics Believe That Isn't in the Bible and Henceforth, Therefore, and So of Course Can't Be True."

And, even with your not-quite-expert knowledge of the Bible, you have to admit — silently to yourself, of course — that your friend seems to have a point.

The words *purgatory* and *Rosary* aren't in the Bible. The Bible does indeed contain verses that on the surface *might* be interpreted as condemnations of calling priests "Father" and having statues (a.k.a. "graven images" — see Commandment No. 2, clause A) in worship spaces.

What's left to be said then? Is your friend right? Since there's lots of Catholic stuff that's not explicitly mentioned in the Bible, and some of it that even seems (notice I said *seems*) to be forbidden by Scripture — and the Bible should be the source of Christian faith — is there indeed something wrong with and somehow less-than-Christian about the Catholic Church?

Be logical here and don't get nervous. How could that be true, anyway? After all, the Catholic Church has been around for two thousand years. Would folks like St. Francis of Assisi and Mother Teresa be so foolish as to be taken in by the nefarious claims of a non-biblical religion cleverly masquerading as Christianity?

What in the world is a good Catholic kid to do?

Question Authority

That is, the authority your friend is presenting to you is the authority you should be questioning. No, not the Bible itself as the Word of God, but her assumptions about what role it plays as an authority for Christian belief.

Is it really true that the Bible is the *only* source of the Christian faith?

Do her own, proudly waved "Bible-only" beliefs even stand up to that claim?

Let's just go ahead and see, okay?

Rather than giving you the answers right at the beginning, let's have you work through this step by step, just as you're going to ask your friend to do. It will stick better that way.

The first question to ask is really, really simple.

Okay, friend, you're claiming that the Bible is the only source of what a Christian should believe. Nothing else — the teachings of Church councils, the wisdom of hundreds of years of Church experience and thought – none of it means anything in terms of basic Christian teachings. God spoke through the Bible and nowhere else. It's in the Bible or it's out.

Where, exactly, in the Bible does it say that?

Where is the verse that states that Christian belief is based *only* on the Bible?

Well?

We're waiting.

And, my friend, we'll be waiting for a very long time. Do you know why?

Because there is no such Bible verse, anywhere in the Bible.

Oh, there are lots of verses about the Scriptures being *a* source of faith, wisdom, inspiration, and, of course, the Word of God – and you'll probably hear them all in answer to this question. But listen carefully to those verses and push your friend on their meaning. None of them – not one single solitary verse anywhere in the whole Bible – explicitly states that the Bible is the *only* source of faith for a Christian or the *only* way that God has revealed Himself.

Let's take a look at a verse that your friend will probably share with you in defense of her Bible-only belief. It's in St. Paul's Second Letter to Timothy: "All scripture is inspired by God and is useful for teaching, for refutation, for correction, and for training in righteousness" (3:16).

It's a fine verse, you have to admit. Paul helpfully reminds Timothy, one of his friends and fellow missionaries, of the importance of Scripture in a life of faith.

But does this passage really say that Scripture is the *only* source that's useful for all those great purposes? Of course it doesn't. If your friend tries to twist the verse so it does read that way, ask her how, exactly, she can claim to read the Bible literally in terms of its plain meaning (a whole other matter, which we'll cover a chapter or two down the road) when she insists on reinterpreting the absolutely plain meaning of a verse to get the meaning *she* wants out of it.

It will be the same with any other verse she can bring out. Don't worry. Just read the verses carefully along with her, but read them for what they say, not for what she's telling you they say.

So here's where our first point leads us: Nowhere in the Bible does it say that the Bible is the *only* place God reveals His truth to us. Nowhere.

That wasn't hard, was it? And to think you were actually nervous about this whole explaining-the-faith thing.

Now let's explore another fun fact. Ask gently — but do ask — the following question. It's a really interesting one, if you think about it: How do we know exactly *what the Bible is?*

I mean, there we have it, those seventy-three books (sixty-six for the Protestants, but we'll get to that little can of worms later) that are supposedly all we need to fully understand the Christian faith.

Well, if the Bible is all we need, then surely the Bible will tell us what books are in it — and I don't mean the table of contents, either, but somewhere in the text, right?

But it's not there. We know, moreover, that the Bible wasn't just dropped from heaven. Even your fundamentalist friend will admit this: The books of the Bible were written and collected over a period of thousands of years. Along the way, there were discussions and disputes within both Judaism and Christianity regarding this very issue: Which books are inspired? Which books are the Word of God, and which aren't?

Again, the broken record starts its merry song:

Where in the Bible does it say what books should be in the Bible? If the Bible is all we need, shouldn't the Bible tell us what's in the Bible?

If the Bible doesn't tell us what should be contained in it, how did we ever find out?

> **If the Bible alone is God's word, God's only revelation of supernatural character, then the Bible will surely say so.**
>
> **Msgr. John J. Glenn,** *Apologetics*

A Few Other Minor Points

Before we get to the positive, very good news that our Catholic faith has to deliver in answer to these seemingly thorny conundrums, let's look at a few other fun questions you can pose to your "Bible-only" friend.

Hey, friend, if an individual's faith is supposed to come from the Bible alone and nothing else, what in the world did Christians do before the printing press was invented?

Johannes Gutenberg produced the first book from a moveable-type printing press around the year 1453. Before that, books, including the Bible of course, had to be hand-copied and were very rare, found only in rich people's houses, universities, and monastery libraries.

What were ordinary, poor Christians to do about faith when, through no fault of their own, Bibles simply weren't available to them?

Even after the invention of the printing press and the mass production of books, relatively few people had entire copies of the Bible in their homes, and the vast majority of people in what we call pre-modern Europe were illiterate. That means they couldn't read any book, including the Bible.

So if all of this Bible-only stuff is true, it really is perfectly reasonable for you to ask some questions of your friend who believes it:

Why would God — a good, fair, and just God, of course — design a system in which the only true knowledge about Him (and, therefore, salvation) would come through means that were impossible for most people to personally encounter through most of Christian history?

Why would God declare that the only way to find out the truth about Him was for individuals to read and reflect on a book that hardly any of them would ever see during their lives (and if they did happen to spy one in church or on a table in the duke's manor, they wouldn't be able to read it anyway)?

Does this make any sense at all?

Does it?

Drum Roll, Please

We've asked a lot of questions, and, as usual, they've left us with even more.

Nowhere in the Bible does it say that the Bible is the sole source of faith.

Nowhere in the Bible does it say exactly what books are or aren't in the Bible.

It doesn't make any sense for God to say that the only way to know about Him and find salvation is through the Bible, which most of the millions of Christians through thousands of years of history never even had a chance to read, simply because illiteracy and the absence of any mass-production book technology made it impossible.

Could there, might there, can there possibly be something else? Something that, alongside and with the Bible, offers us God's complete revelation and truth?

Well, I'm glad that you asked, because there is such a thing.

It's called Church.

It's called Tradition.

It's called the Other Half of the Picture.

Now, the first thing to do when you're trying to understand this is to get straight in your mind exactly what we mean when we say "Church." We're speaking of something broader than your parish, something even bigger than the Catholic Church in the twenty-first century.

We're talking about the Body of Christ — the presence on earth of Jesus, here and with us now, just as He had promised His apostles. For you see, it all comes down to this; and this might be a little hard for your friend to swallow, but it's the absolute truth.

Jesus, upon His ascension into heaven, didn't leave a Bible behind. He left a Church. He left a group of eleven men who had listened to Him preach and teach for three years, a group that would be empowered a few days later on Pentecost, to go out and preach, teach, and heal just as He had done, spreading that very true, very powerful, and very Good News.

Christianity grew in those early days because of the teaching and preaching of those apostles. It grew because of the presence of Jesus they brought to communities through prayer, baptism, and celebrations of the Eucharist — and all of this without a word of the New Testament having been written down.

Eventually, of course, the Good News was committed to paper — or parchment or vellum, to be more accurate. Beginning around the year 56, Paul's letters, then the Gospels, some other letters, and finally, by the end of the first century, the Book of Revelation had all been written and were slowly being circulated among Christian communities.

But you can be sure that even then, and well into the fourth century, few Christian communities had the benefit of seeing all of those books we now call the New Testament at one time. Some communities in some towns might have copies of one Gospel and maybe a couple of Paul's letters. Some lucky communities might have had more.

So the truth — the real, historical truth — is that Christianity grew and spread like wildfire in those first few centuries, not because people were sitting around reading the Bible, but because the Church — in the person of apostles, preachers, and teachers — came to their communities and taught what the apostles had been taught by Christ Himself, bringing that Good News of salvation and celebrating it in what we now call the "sacraments."

> **The gift of God was entrusted to the church that all the members might receive of Him and be alive.**
>
> ST. IRENAEUS,
> *Adversus Omnes Haereses*

Here's the point: The Church came before the New Testament. (You can say that about the Old Testament as well. Hardly any of it was actually written down before the ninth century B.C. But did that mean that the Jewish people didn't experience God's revelation of Himself before that point? How absurd is that?)

The Bible, as we have it today — those specific books, and no others — grew *out of the Church*, not the other way around. It was the Church, through councils of bishops meeting in the fourth century, guided by the Holy Spirit, that determined which of the many books floating around claiming to be the inspired Word of God actually were inspired.

Do you see how logical all this is?

And this is exactly what Catholics believe about the whole matter of Scripture, Tradition, and faith — this logical, historically reasonable truth (we'll let the *Catechism of the Catholic Church* take it from here):

> "Sacred Tradition and Sacred Scripture make up a single sacred deposit of the Word of God," in which,

as in a mirror, the pilgrim Church contemplates God, the source of all her riches. (No. 97)

This very complete, holistic view of faith and truth explains a lot that the fundamentalist view just ignores. It's rooted in a clearer sense of what Jesus actually did and left behind to carry on His ministry. It takes the history of Christianity seriously. It addresses the very true fact that although not every tiny aspect of Christian belief is *explicitly stated* in Scripture, it's all *rooted* in the Bible and none of it *contradicts* Scripture either.

So there you go.

Your friend is absolutely right. The Catholic Church isn't a Bible-only church. And to tell the truth, we're pretty happy about that particular state of affairs.

Why?

Oh, I guess because we'd rather base our faith on the whole truth that God has given us, instead of just part of it.

But maybe we're just funny that way.

SO WHAT YOU SAY IS . . .

❑ You're right. Catholic Christianity isn't a Bible-only church. That's because the Scriptures make it clear that God has revealed Himself through *both* the Bible *and* the Sacred Tradition of the Church.

❑ There's not a single place in the Bible that says the Bible should be the only source of faith for Christians, either.

❑ Jesus didn't leave the Bible behind when He ascended into heaven. He left us the Church, in the ministry of His apostles. The Bible emerged from the Church, not the other way around.

THREE

"Why Don't You Read the Bible Literally?"

Do you get it? Do you see what your fundamentalist friend is up to here?

It's pretty simple. He's implying that the only legitimate way to read the Bible is by understanding every word, passage, and story in its "plain, literal sense."

So, of course, since that's not the Catholic position on Scripture interpretation (and it's not), it must follow that Catholics are, therefore, not real, true, authentic, saved Christians.

Wrong.

It's as if someone tells you that since you're a girl, you probably don't have what it takes to succeed in math or science. Or if you hear the argument that because you're a teenager, there's no way you're trustworthy.

What would you do if you were confronted with dumb statements like those? You would question the assumptions, of course.

And that's exactly what we'll do here.

We're not going to accept the fundamentalist's assumptions about how "real" Christians should read and interpret the Bible. We're going to show him that this business of across-the-board literal readings of every single line in the Bible isn't consistent with what the Bible is, or how most Jews and Christians have read and understood it over the centuries.

Best of all, we're going to show him that even he, Mr. Biblical Literalist, doesn't, in fact, practice what he preaches.

What Did You Mean by That?

Let's start by talking about talking, and let's get personal about it.

Think back, if you can, to those days, many years ago, when you were oh-so-young and immature.

Dad passes by your room, observes that you are deeply involved in the intricacies of MultiMindbender 2, but dares to speak anyway.

"Hey there," he says, "Take the trash out, okay?"

Articulate as ever, you answer, "Sure."

Hours pass. Dad passes. The only part of you that's moved in the recent past are your fingers. Dad speaks again, but this time that old joviality is nothing but a faint echo.

"I thought I asked you to take out the trash!"

You turn, blink away the pixels, and answer, quite reasonably, you think, "But you didn't say *when* you wanted me to do it."

It doesn't take Dad long to make his original intentions perfectly clear.

Let's dance across the meadows of memory to another time, perhaps when it was you who was lost in a lousy mood.

After your forty-seventh gripe of the day, dear Mom, in an uncharacteristic departure from her usually sunny demeanor, snaps.

"Oh, just shut your mouth!" she barks.

Moments later, Mom has an occasion to ask you a question, raising her voice above your baby brother's screams in order to be heard.

"Have you seen Cornelius's binky?" she asks in a panic.

Of course you have. You know exactly where it is — you just saw it under the couch when you were looking for your right shoe. But all you're willing to offer right now is a shake of the head and a shrug of your shoulders, pointing helplessly to your tightly clamped lips.

"Mmm mmm m mm mmm m mm MMMMMM!" you smirk. Translation: *You told me to keep my mouth SHUT!*

Ah, isn't it wonderful that human beings are so far evolved beyond the rest of the animal kingdom, and that we just communicate so well?

For you see, these examples offer you nothing less than a mini-course in the wonders and perils of literal understandings of human words.

Your dad didn't think you were quite dense enough to believe that he meant for you to take care of the trash any other time besides that very moment. He didn't think that he had to spell out his expectations in exact literal terms — he assumed that you understood him better than that.

And as for you and that zipped-up mouth of yours — well, two can play at that *Oh-You-Didn't-Mean-that-Literally?* game, you know. Just wait until the next time you ask for some money before you head to the mall, and you watch as Mom drops three pennies, a dime, and a old peso she's still got from that anniversary cruise to Cancún into your anxious little hand.

"You just asked for *some* money. You didn't say *how much* or *what kind*, did you?"

Moms can smirk, too, you've noticed.

It's quite obvious that normal human communication involves quite a bit of non-literal understanding. Sure, we expect a lot of what we say to be taken according to its plain, simple, surface meanings, but have you noticed how much *doesn't*?

For the simple fact is, human beings do not, and never really have, through their entire, lengthy, mysterious history, sat around and simply spoken and heard one another in purely literal terms.

Just think for a minute how much of your own daily communication involves going beyond the literal meaning of words.

Your facial expression when you answer normal questions about your daily well-being: You can say "fine" with a smile, or "fine" with your eyes rolling up to the sky, and convey two completely different states of existence.

The words and phrases you pick to tell a story at lunch: You say biology class "rocked." Did it? Did the classroom really churn back and forth on its foundations, or were you really saying it was great because the teacher was absent and the sub couldn't find the test?

You say that your mom "hit the roof" when you broke curfew. Really? Is she okay now? Does her head still hurt?

A friend glances outside and comments that it's "raining cats and dogs." Oh my! Poor things! But I don't hear them barking, do you?

And then, there's that moment, after school, standing in the almost-empty parking lot with that person you really, really like, that you can't stop thinking about, whose smile makes the sun rise and whose departure from school every afternoon plunges your life into an endless circle of meaninglessness. Somehow, you have to communicate all of this. You open your mouth, and, risking all of your pride and about five-sevenths of your self-esteem, you force the words out.

"Uh – I really – uh – you know, like you."

So you did it. You said those words that were literally true. But do they even come close to conveying what you mean?

So you get it, right? You see that one of the aspects of human communication that makes it so rich and so interesting is the fact that we do, all the time, go beyond the literal meaning of words. We use metaphors, similes, personifications, and all of that other stuff you learned about in English class.

You might have also noticed that the deeper the experience and the more profound the feelings we're trying to express, the less adequate purely literal language is to get the message across. It would be an incredibly boring world if all human beings did to communicate was to sit around and speak in plain, literal terms to one another.

Truth, if you must know, is a lot deeper than words. This may seem like a roundabout way of getting back to our fundamentalist friends' objection, but it's really not.

For, you see, Catholics (and most other Christians, to tell the truth) *do* understand the Bible to be the Word of God — inspired, revealed, and truthful — but that *doesn't* mean we're called to read every word of the Word literally. Because, to put it quite simply, that's not the way human beings communicate.

God used human beings to write His Word. God used all the incredible variety of written communication those human authors had at their fingertips and within their cultures to get that Word across.

So, we effortlessly conclude, if we're not limited to literal understandings in our own communication, why would God be?

The truth is, He's not.

What's the Bible, Anyway?

See, this is what's going on when your fundamentalist friend tries to back you up against the Wall of Biblical Literalism. He's pushed you into accepting his basic assumption that since the Bible is God's Word, the only acceptable way to read it is literally.

And that's just not the case.

In fact, that particular conviction — that the entire Bible should be read literally — is a pretty recent one. For centuries (check that — millennia), Jews and Christians who've read and studied the Word of God have understood that it contains layers and layers of meanings that go way beyond the literal, and are sometimes even hidden by it.

You really should point this out to your friend, too: The Bible is not, contrary to popular belief, a single book. It's a collection of seventy-three books written over hundreds of years. This collection contains many different kinds of books composed in various literary styles and forms. It has poetry (Psalms) and history (lots of books, including, but not limited to, books like Exodus, Judges, and 1 and 2 Samuel). It has legal material (filling up most of Leviticus). It has government records (Numbers). It has short stories (Tobit). It has truth wrapped up in ancient tribal stories (parts of Genesis). It has prophecy, proverbs, and letters. And it has this unique form of biography found nowhere else in human literature — these books we call "Gospels."

It's obvious to anyone who takes time to flip through the pages of this amazing set of books we call Scripture that God was not limited to one single style of expression as He revealed Himself. He also obviously knew that human beings want and even need to go beyond one particular style. We have imaginations and deep, deep spirits, made in His image, that are capable of so much more.

> **Every Christian must refer always and everywhere to Scriptures for all his choices . . . not daring to take a step without being illuminated by the divine rays of those words.**
>
> **POPE JOHN PAUL II**

So reading the entire Bible as if every word of it is nothing more than plain-as-day statements and propositions — with no historical context, no variation in literary form, and no connection to an author's intent — is about as smart as walking into your school library and reading Emily Dickinson the same way you read a history of the Battle of the Bulge. Both contain truth; but if you try to get at the truth in the same way for both, you end up missing it.

And please, as you discuss these matters, don't forget to ask your friend our very most favorite question of all: "Where in the Bible does it say that the only way to read the entire Bible is literally?"

Answer: Nowhere. Let's move on.

How to Tell What Is True

Let's get at this another way.

All facts are true. But not all truth can be or even needs to be expressed as literal fact. And please memorize this and never forget it:

If truth is expressed in non-literal ways, it's still true.

We are not saying here that because the human authors of the Bible used lots of metaphors, lots of different literary forms, and even very consciously told fictional stories sometimes, that there are parts of the Bible that aren't "true."

NO!

The whole Bible *is* true. It's just that God chose to express His Word in various ways: sometimes in ways that we should read and understand as literal fact, and sometimes in poetry, metaphor, and stories.

Just to put things straight, let's lay out what the *Catechism of the Catholic Church* teaches about the truth of Scripture:

"The Sacred Scriptures contain the Word of God and, because they are inspired, they are truly the Word of God." (No. 135)

God is the author of Sacred Scripture because he inspired its human authors; he acts in them and by
means of them. He thus gives assurance that their writings teach without error his saving truth. (No. 136)

It's clear, isn't it, that Catholics believe that the Bible is
the inspired Word of God? The difference between us and
the fundamentalist Christian is that we believe that God
used all kinds of human expression — not just the bald-
faced, plain-as-day, literal kind — to get His point across.

One More Thing

I have to admit that this is my favorite part. This is the
part where we get to show the person who claims that literal interpretation is the only way to read the Bible that he,
in fact, doesn't follow his own rules. Maybe it's wrong to
enjoy this part so much. But, you know, that's just too bad.

Get a Bible. Not some gooney paraphrase translation
or a "youth Bible," but a good, solid translation like the
New American Bible or the Revised Standard Version
(Catholic edition). Open the Bible to Matthew 26 and have
your friend read verses 26 through 28 out loud. In case you
haven't figure it out yet, it's one of the accounts of the Last
Supper.

Now, ask your friend, very politely, what happened to
the bread and wine over which Jesus spoke those words.
Did they literally become His body and blood?

I will guarantee you that your friend will say no. He'll
say that Jesus was speaking metaphorically, that He was
saying that the bread and wine should *remind* the apostles
of His body and blood.

Ask why your friend has, all of a sudden, decided not to read part of God's Word literally. After all, the meaning is very plain, even in the original Greek: "Is" is the word used. And if your friend doubts you, ask why the apostle Paul, writing a couple of decades after the Last Supper, obviously understood Jesus' words in their literal sense. In Paul's First Letter to the Corinthians, he says:

> *The cup of blessing that we bless, is it not a participation*
> *in the blood of Christ? The bread that we break, is it not*
> *a participation in the body of Christ?* (10:16)

Now, I promise that your friend will try to dance around this by saying that Paul was, like Jesus, using symbolic language. (I'll forgive you if you find yourself stammering in disbelief at this point. I always do.)

"How in the world," you're perfectly justified in asking, "is saying that Jesus and Paul were speaking symbolically a literal reading of the Bible? It's not. You are, my friend, interpreting, and not in any way sticking with the plain, obvious meaning of the words."

So here it is: Your friend will fight about Adam and Eve and seven days of creation for hours, implying that if you don't read those passages as literal accounts of history, you're not Christian. But then, when faced with the plain literal words of Jesus, presented by the Gospel writers and Paul as simple historical recollection — and understood in their plain sense by the early Christians, I might add — he'll dance and sing that old fundamentalist song that you're going to hear quite a bit; a song I like to call "It Means What It Says — Except When I Don't Want It To!"

SO WHAT YOU SAY IS . . .

❏ Catholics believe that the Bible is God's Word, trust-worthy and true, God's revelation of Himself.

❏ Because God worked through human authors, the Bible conveys truth in a variety of literary styles, many of which are intended to be understood literally, others not.

❏ There's not a single verse in the Bible that demands that the whole Bible be understood literally, without interpretation.

❏ No matter what literary form is used, God's truth is still present.

❏ There are many passages throughout the Bible that fundamentalists don't take literally. This shows pretty clearly that (a) literal interpretation is inconsistently applied and (b) is used to defend already-held beliefs, rather than objectively uncover the truth of Scripture.

FOUR

"Why Aren't Some of Your Beliefs in the Bible?"

Hey! Haven't we been here before? As in a couple of chapters ago?

I just can't get anything past you. You're right — in Chapter Two, we looked at the fundamentalists' accusation that because Catholicism isn't a "Bible-only" church, it can't possibly be authentically Christian. We quite skillfully dismantled that illusion, right then and there. So what else is there to say?

A lot. In that previous chapter, we took a good look at the Bible-only belief in principle, and we saw how it's built on the sand of historical misunderstandings — and lot of very selective reading, to boot. We even made the astonishing discovery that the Bible-only concept can't be found in the Bible at all.

So you've got the abstractions down, and you also understand how your Catholic Tradition interprets Scripture. Good. Now we're ready to take all that useful knowledge and apply it to specific issues that your friend is bound to bring up. We know that she will, because fundamentalist anti-Catholic tracts spill over with gleeful accusations about all of this stuff.

This is the basic slam you're going to hear:

> "The Catholic Church is built on man-made traditions, not the Word of God."

Now, there are several possible responses to this:

"Oh really? Do tell me more."

"So? What of it?"

Or you could just say, "Do you really have any clue at all as to what you're talking about?"

Of course, you would say it a lot more nicely than that.

But your point would be the same: to explain to your friend that, yes, the Catholic faith is built on the dual foundation of Scripture *and* Tradition.

But you know what? That's not a bad thing. In fact, when you take a good, honest look at Scripture and the real, actual history of Christianity, it's the way of looking at what Jesus left behind in this Church that actually makes the most sense.

You've already begun explaining Tradition to your friend back when you went over the inadequacy of the whole Bible-only concept, but now's the perfect time to go into a little more depth.

Your first job is to help your friend understand what Catholics mean when we talk about *Tradition*.

You notice that's "Tradition" with a capital "T," not "traditions." There's a reason for that, and the reason is that Tradition and traditions are two different things.

Traditions are, to put it briefly, habitual human practices. Every time human beings stick together in a group for more than an hour, they somehow, for some reason, develop traditions.

Your family probably has traditions regarding everything from who takes out the trash to how your parents say good-night to you — or, should I say, *used* to say good-night to you, you all-too-cool, super-independent dude, you!

Your school is probably bubbling with traditions, some of them totally meaningless and others that actually bear some significance and might even bring a tear to your eye if you're not careful.

Sure enough, traditions are all over the place – even in Bible-only churches, I'll bet. Ask your friend if every service at her church is completely created from scratch every week, with absolutely no relation to what went on before. No? Uh-oh – nailed you, buddy! Man-made traditions are there, it's clear to see.

That's what traditions are, and every human institution has them, because human beings derive meaning and security from traditions – Catholics included, of course. The practice of saying the Rosary is a tradition, as is crossing yourself with holy water as you enter a church. A May Crowning is a tradition and so is the Jesse Tree. Our faith isn't built *on* these traditions; traditions grow *out of* our faith.

Now, *Tradition* is something else, something deeper, and just a little less concrete. As we hinted at back in Chapter Two, Catholics see Tradition as one of the two primary ways God has revealed Himself to us, along with His Word in the Scriptures.

Remember how we said Jesus didn't leave a book behind when He ascended into heaven? What was it He did leave?

He left, of course, His teaching, which was heard and taken to heart by the apostles, whom He, in turn, very solemnly commissioned to go out and share the Good News with the entire world (see Matthew 28:18-20 and Acts 1:7-8).

That's Tradition — to be more specific, we Catholics call it "Sacred Tradition" or even "Apostolic Tradition." It's the teaching that Jesus entrusted to the apostles, which they, in turn, handed down to their successors, the bishops, who are responsible for sharing it with the entire Church.

So, here's the first step in your answer: Sure enough, the Church is built on God's Word, but it's built on the *entirety* of God's Word: both the

> **Through Tradition, "the Church, in her doctrine, life, and worship perpetuates and transmits to every generation all that she herself is, all that she believes. . . . And the Holy Spirit, through whom the living voice of the Gospel rings out in the Church — and through her in the world — leads believers to the full truth, and makes the Word of Christ dwell in them in all its richness."**
>
> *CATECHISM OF THE CATHOLIC CHURCH*
> **(Nos. 78-79)**

Holy Scriptures and the Sacred Tradition handed down by the apostles, who received it from Jesus Himself.

In other words, the Catholic faith is not built on "man-made" traditions. It's built on the Word that God has given to us through Scripture and Sacred Tradition.

Ask your friend, "Can you tell me exactly why you think that's a bad thing?"

Tradition in Scripture

Now, we're not a Bible-only faith, but your friend is arguing from that perspective. So, as you go through this thorny topic, it's only right to alert you to what Scripture says about all of this, so you'll be prepared.

The Greek word that's the equivalent of our English word *tradition* is *paradosis*. We find this word used a lot in the New Testament, in both positive and negative senses. Let's take care of the negative stuff first, because that, without doubt, is where your friend is going to go, and quickly, too:

> See to it that no one captivate you with an empty, seductive philosophy according to human tradition, according to the elemental powers of the world and not according to Christ. (COLOSSIANS 2:8)

Here, Paul warns the Colossian Christians to be careful about false teaching. Why? Because in these early days of Christianity (very early — about twenty years after the Resurrection), there were lots of competing ideas about what "real" faith in Jesus was all about. Some things never change, do they?

There were those who felt pretty strongly that Christians should still observe the whole Jewish Law. There were also lots of pagan philosophies and religious systems floating around, offering various kinds of salvation to anyone who would listen.

Paul's warning is about all of those "traditions" — both the Jewish traditions, which he felt the New Covenant had put in the past, and the traditions of human, pagan philosophy. Here's another one, from Jesus Himself:

> *"You disregard God's commandment but cling to human tradition. . . . You nullify the word of God in favor of your tradition that you have handed on."* (Mark 7:8, 13)

If you read the whole passage, you'll see that Jesus' words here are in response to Pharisees and scribes who were criticizing Him for not really caring whether His disciples ate without ritually purifying themselves first. Jesus' response is clear: Those traditions have nothing to do with salvation, nothing to do with holiness, and nothing to do with being loved and treasured by the Father.

Now think about all of that, and work this out along with me.

Neither Paul nor Jesus is talking about Tradition with a capital "T," are they? They're both talking about human traditions that might have begun as legitimate expressions of faith but, as time went on, outlived their usefulness — and which could even become obstacles to faith.

In other words, they're not talking about the Sacred Tradition entrusted by Jesus to His apostles.

By now, you won't be surprised to learn that every scriptural mention of what we understand as Sacred Tradition is positive:

> *Therefore, brothers, stand firm and hold fast to the traditions that you were taught, either by an oral statement or by a letter of ours.* (2 THESSALONIANS 2:15)

> *I praise you because you remember me in everything and hold fast to the traditions, just as I handed them on to you.* (1 CORINTHIANS 11:2)

Now, you always have to be careful using Bible verses in these discussions. People have observed that you can prove almost anything — including an opposing viewpoint — from Scripture, and they're right about that. But what we've done here is a lot more than swap Bible verses. We've shown our fundamentalist friend that the evidence from the Bible indicates very clearly that the apostles passed on the faith orally, at first, and only later by the written Word we now call the Bible. They accepted that oral tradition as a valid way of passing on the faith they had been taught by Jesus and had experienced in His presence.

And do you know what? Catholics still do!

Here We Go Again

Once again, we've reached the part of this discussion that is my personal favorite: showing the fundamentalist Christian how her critique of Catholicism can be turned right around and applied to her very own church.

Let's take the "man-made traditions" thing first.

You friend might point out all kinds of elements of Catholicism that are, she says, of human origin and not explicitly described and okayed in the Bible. She'll talk about the pope. She'll talk about rosaries and Mary and praying to saints. She'll talk about purgatory, and she might even talk about the Mass.

In general, what you will do is show that while none of those elements of our faith are explicitly mentioned in the Bible, none of them are *anti-biblical*, either. None of them contradict God's Word as He's given it to us in Scripture. Later chapters of this book give you help in dealing with each specific topic.

But you will also want to ask your friend to take a good look at her own church and her own denomination. Is every single aspect of her church's life explicitly described in the Bible?

Where in the Bible does it say that a church should have something called a "youth minister?"

Where in the Bible does it say that a church service should have the particular shape and structure that her church has?

In fact, you could very legitimately ask, where in the Bible does it say that preaching should be at the center of a Christian worship service, as it is in most evangelical churches? The Acts of the Apostles and Paul's First Letter to the Corinthians both indicate that for the early Christians, the Eucharist was the center of worship life — every single week.

Why doesn't her church do what Scripture says on that score, instead of depending on man-made structures for worship?

And speaking of man-made, ask your friend (nicely now) who the founder of her denomination is. If she doesn't know, ask her to do some research on it. The answers you're going to get won't get any earlier than the sixteenth century, and every possible denomination you're going to encounter was brought into existence by a human being — be that person Martin Luther, John Calvin, John Wesley, or some Spirit-filled folks in early twentieth-century California (the Pentecostal churches).

To whom do we trace the origins of the Catholic Church?

Not a mere man, we're happy to say. More like The Man: Jesus Christ.

So whose church is rooted in man-made traditions?

SO WHAT YOU SAY IS . . .

❑ All human organizations have traditions: families, schools, clubs, and even churches of all denominations.

❑ The Catholic Church values traditions that grow out of authentic faith, but it isn't "built on" such traditions.

❑ The Catholic Church is built on Jesus Christ. Jesus promised He would be with the Church always, and we believe Him.

❑ The Catholic Church is built on the truth and power of God's revelations as proclaimed in His complete Word, contained in both Scripture and Tradition.

❑ Negative mentions of "tradition" in the New Testament always refer to practices that weren't rooted in authentic faith or had strayed from it.

❑ "Tradition" is mentioned positively many times in the New Testament. The apostles — including Paul — spoke of Tradition as a primary way they passed on the Good News about Jesus.

FIVE

"Why Doesn't Your Church
Let You Interpret Scripture?"

What in the world is your friend talking about here?

Of course, you, as a happening Catholic young person, can read the Bible on your own. Of course, your Bible doesn't come complete with a booklet called "This Is What the Bible Means — And Don't You Dare Think for Yourself. Love, The Pope."

What does your friend mean that Catholics don't interpret Scripture for themselves and need the Church to do it for them? Then what in the world have you been doing in all those religion classes, where you spent hours and hours and hours discussing, writing, and reflecting on the question that recently won the award of Most Frequently Asked in Religion Textbooks: "Explain what this Scripture passage means to you"?

Time for a history lesson. Sorry, but it's completely necessary, and it won't take long. It's all about that fairly important event called the Protestant Reformation.

We've spoken of the Protestant Reformation before, and it will come up again. You know from your history classes that we trace the main road of the Reformation back to a Catholic monk named Martin Luther.

Martin Luther had a lot of ideas, but central to most of them were those familiar ones you've already heard in this book and some we'll be discussing in upcoming chapters:

- That the Bible is the sole source of authority for the Christian faith.
- That human beings are saved by the grace of God alone, not by their own efforts.
- That God speaks primarily through an individual's conscience and reading of Scripture, not through the Tradition and teachings of the Church. An individual's reading of Scripture has more authority than Church doctrine.

Ah ha! Now you see where your friend is coming from. For that last focus of the Protestant Reformation — the primacy of an individual's reading of Scripture — has remained, over the past five centuries, central to all Protestant faiths.

Which is, we might add, exactly why there are literally thousands of different Protestant denominations now. But we'll have more to say on that later.

So . . . Is It True?

Is what your fundamentalist friend saying true? Are Catholics discouraged from interpreting Scripture on their own?

Of course not.

A simple eye-opening excursion out of Fundamentalist Fantasy Land into the reality of Catholicism will demonstrated this fact to your friends in a pretty concrete way.

Catholic bookstores are filled with Bibles and Bible-study guides.

Almost every Catholic parish features adult Bible study as part of its education program.

This one's easy, and one you can talk about from your own experience (I hope!): Catholic-school religion courses all, without exception, include lessons on the Bible. If you've attended parish religious education, you've studied Scripture there, too.

Finally, grab a missal booklet from church (just return it next week, okay?), and take a little trip through the order of the Mass with your fundamentalist friend. Point out all the many, many places in the Mass that are all about Scripture and little else:

- The *Gloria* begins with the angels' announcement from Luke 2:14.
- During Sunday Mass, we hear three readings from Scripture *and* we sing one of the psalms as a response between the first and second readings.
- The *Sanctus* (or "Holy, Holy, Holy") that we sing or recite before the eucharistic prayer is rooted in passages from Revelation 4:7-11 as well as the part of Psalm 118 (25-26) that the crowds sang to Jesus as He arrived in Jerusalem.
- And then, of course, there's that whole matter of the consecration from the eucharistic prayer, taken directly from Jesus' words in the Gospels, repeated and celebrated just as He asked us to.

So after this little flood of new and startling information, your friend should have no doubt that Catholics are encouraged to read the Bible, are given the means to study the Bible on their own by their parishes and schools, and are immersed in the Bible every single time they go to Mass. If your friend won't see those simple, really obvious points, she's obviously lost the key that opens up her mind, and I feel really, really sorry for you.

Now, what about that whole conflict between an individual's interpretation of Scripture and the Church's? Your fundamentalist friend seems to think that the Catholic Church's emphasis on Church and Tradition puts an unnecessary and even soul-threatening obstacle between a believer and God. Does it?

As in paradise, God walks in the Holy Scriptures, seeking man.

ST. AMBROSE,
Epistle 49,3

The Church recognizes that an individual's faith is all about a living relationship with Jesus Christ. That faith is nourished and shaped by both Sacred Tradition and Sacred Scripture. Both are equally important.

The Church also knows that the Scriptures are boundless in the nourishment they provide. You can read the Scriptures at many different levels of understanding. The same passage will resonate with you differently at different points in your life.

So, with the richness of God's Word in Scripture in mind, the Church does not — and I want to emphasize DOES NOT — waste its time dictating what every passage in the Bible means to the exclusion of all meanings. There is no such thing as an *official Catholic interpretation of the Bible*.

No, the Church's role in biblical interpretation is, to tell the truth, more negative in its emphasis. That means that there are times in which a really strange or obviously wrong interpretation of a Bible passage will become popular.

For example, some people will interpret what Paul says about marriage in 1 Corinthians 7:8 ("Now to the unmarried and to widows, I say: it is a good thing for them to remain as they are, as I do. . . .") as a reason to run around telling everyone that marriage is a bad thing. (This has really happened at various times in Church history.)

At that point, the Church — usually in the person of a bishop (remember that the bishops are our primary teachers and the heirs to the apostles) — will step in and say, "Uh-oh. That's not what that passage means. You're misusing it and twisting it, and refusing to see that particular passage in the context in which it was written." Or something like that, in a lot fancier language.

Do you get it?

So often, people outside the Church see its teaching role as involving nothing but handing down lots of doctrines we just gotta believe or else. The fact is, a vital part of the Church's teaching ministry (a responsibility given by

Jesus Himself, remember?) is the very useful and necessary task of putting the brakes on misinterpretations of
Scripture that might be about to lead its followers into a
faith that's barely even Christian.

The Consequences of Individual Interpretation

So, yeah, sure, Catholics believe that God speaks to us
individually through His Word every time we hear and read
it. But we also believe that the teaching authority of the
Church is important. Why? Because it's an authority given
by Jesus. It's a gift to help us keep on track.

And look what happens without that gift.

It might be a rather delicate subject, but you really should
push your fundamentalist friend on the consequences of this
emphasis on individual interpretation of Scripture.

Just go to the reference section of your library and find
an encyclopedia or dictionary of Christian denominations.
Start counting how many different Protestant denominations there are.

I'll come back tomorrow and see how you're doing.

For the fact is, there are literally thousands of them,
almost every one of them split off from another Protestant
denomination because some people in the original church
disagreed with other people's "individual interpretation"
of Scripture so much that they formed their own church
centered around their own "individual interpretation."

This is the point at which, to be perfectly frank about
it, the fundamentalist theory — from biblical literalism to
individual interpretation to Bible-only authority — completely breaks down.

IF the Bible has such a plain, literal meaning, why doesn't everyone who individually interprets it see it exactly the same way?

WHY would God want us to rely only on ourselves to interpret the Bible when it obviously and invariably leads to a riot of different opinions, and then to different churches, all preaching different versions of truth?

WHY would God leave us His Word in such a complex book as the Bible without leaving us a trustworthy helper in interpreting it?

It should be absolutely clear by now that He didn't. It should be absolutely clear that if this is the point at which the fundamentalist *theory* breaks down, it's also the point at which the Catholic *reality* comes together in a perfectly reasonable way.

For here's what the real historical evidence points to: God *didn't* leave us all alone to struggle, to interpret His Word all by ourselves. Jesus very clearly left with the apostles that great gift: the Holy Spirit, present in the Church, teaching, helping us to understand, and guarding us from error — not to speak of innumerable church divisions.

After all, do you know what it says in — ahem — the Bible?

In the Acts of the Apostles (8:26-39), the apostle Philip has just met an Ethiopian court official on the road. The Ethiopian is riding along, reading the Jewish Scriptures. Philip asks him, "Do you understand what you are reading?"

The Ethiopian answers Philip, quite reasonably, "How can I, unless someone instructs me?"

An excellent question, don't you agree?

SO WHAT YOU SAY IS . . .

❏ Of course Catholics are encouraged to read the Bible and depend on it for spiritual guidance and God's Word.

❏ The Catholic Church has "officially" interpreted very few passages of the Bible. Most of the time, the Church's role in biblical interpretation is to clarify what a passage *doesn't* mean.

❏ This clarifying role is very important. It is the gift of discerning and preaching the truth that was given by Jesus to the apostles. It was given to safe-guard the truth of the Gospel and the unity of the Church.

❏ Dependence on "individual interpretation" invariably leads to division in the Body of Christ.

SIX

"Why Has Your Church Added Books to the Bible?"

Are you getting tired of being put on the defensive? Too bad, because we're nowhere near finished yet.

There is, you know, a solution close at hand when you're feeling besieged.

Refuse to *be* on the defensive. Your fundamentalist friend's questions implicitly assume the incorrectness of Catholicism. Don't accept that assumption. As you think about these questions, get to the answer, certainly, but get there in a positive spirit — have confidence that there's not even the tiniest element of these Catholic beliefs that is in the least anti-Christian. You've got two thousand years of Tradition (yes, the one with a capital "T"!) behind you. Have confidence in that.

And don't forget, once you're finished explaining, to ask, every time: "Well, since we see that this Catholic belief fits in just fine with the teachings of Scripture and Christian Tradition, can you explain to me why you *don't* believe it?"

The Bible is a great place to start — because, you know, your friend is right. The Catholic and Protestant Bibles are different, and here's how.

A Catholic version of the Bible contains several Old Testament books that are absent from the Protestant version. These books are:

- Tobit

- 1 and 2 Maccabees
- Wisdom
- Sirach
- Baruch

Besides that, there are sections of both Esther and Daniel that you'll find in the Catholic Bible and not in the Protestant.

We call these books the *deuterocanonical* books. Protestants refer to them as the *Apocrypha*, which comes from a Greek word meaning "hidden," and in normal usage implies inauthenticity.

So why is this? Did we add books? Did the Protestants take them away? What gives?

How It Happened

It's really not that complicated.

You know by now that the process of bringing the books of the Bible together was a long one, lasting thousands of years.

By the time of Jesus, there were a few translations of the various books of the Hebrew Scriptures circulating around the ancient Near East — people spoke different languages, so, just like today, translations were necessary.

The version that Jesus and His apostles knew, studied, and used more than any other was called the *Septuagint*. It was a Greek translation of the Hebrew Scriptures.

Now, the Septuagint (so named for the legendary seventy — get that root prefix *sept* — Jewish scholars who translated it) contained all of the books that today you would find in the Old Testament of a Catholic Bible — every one of those books, including those that are not in the Protestant version.

Around the year 90, Jewish-Christian relations had deteriorated to a terribly low level. Up to this time, of course, many Christians still considered themselves Jews — just Jews who believed that the Messiah had come in the person of Jesus of Nazareth.

By the end of the first century, clear divisions had evolved, and Jewish leaders determined that it was indeed blasphemous to hold these beliefs about Jesus. So around this time, a couple of things happened: Christians were officially banned from Jewish synagogues; and in a gathering in the year 90, in a town called Javneh, Jewish rabbis clarified what, for them, was Scripture.

They excluded the Gospels, of course, as well as many other books. Included in those books were the unique books of the Hebrew Scriptures that were found in the Septuagint translation and not in many others — those seven we listed above, plus sections of Esther and Daniel. These leaders weren't happy with the Septuagint because it was the translation of the Bible that Christians tended to use when defending and explaining their beliefs.

So that was that, as far as Judaism was concerned.

But you notice where that leaves Christianity — *with* the Septuagint, *with* the complete Hebrew Scriptures, including those disputed seven books.

And this is where Christianity left it for about one thousand four hundred years — until the Protestant Reformation. The simple truth is, for about fifteen hundred years, the Christian Church used the "Catholic" version of the Bible.

Then along came Martin Luther, determined to prove that his doctrine of "faith alone" was true, even if he had to take books out of the Bible to do it.

Sorry to be so harsh, but that's really what happened.

What Luther did was this: When he translated the Bible into German, he took out those seven disputed books and put them in an appendix at the back of the Old Testament. He did the same thing with Hebrews, James, Jude, and Revelation in the New Testament.

All of these books contain passages that dispute Luther's concept of faith, as well as support certain Catholic teachings that he said were wrong. For example, he removed 2 Maccabees because it contains verses (12:41-45) that support the Catholic teaching on purgatory!

He and later Protestant Reformers supported removing these books from the Old Testament because, they said, if Jews didn't have use for them, then they couldn't be valid. In saying this, they completely ignored some plain historical facts that you yourself just mastered a few paragraphs ago: Jews *did* see these books as inspired up until the year 90. Jesus and the apostles used the Septuagint version of the Bible themselves, and there are even quotations from the deuterocanonical books scattered throughout the New Testament.

So, do you see now how, once you know the facts, the question takes on a whole different meaning?

Your fundamentalist friend has been taught the untruth that the Catholic Church "added" books to the Bible. That's simply not true, is it? What really happened is that the Protestant Reformers *removed* books from the canon of the Bible that had been accepted by all Christians everywhere for hundreds of years, simply to fit their own theological agenda.

Looking at it this way, in the context of those inconvenient things called facts, it's perfectly legitimate to turn the question around and ask your friend, to answer in all honesty: "So, tell me again — Why doesn't your church use the version of the Bible that Jesus and the apostles used? Why is it that your church doesn't use the *whole* Bible?"

SO WHAT YOU SAY IS . . .

❑ Catholics have used the same Bible for about two thousand years.

❑ The Catholic Bible is rooted in the Septuagint, the version of the Bible used by many Jews in the ancient world — including Jesus, the apostles, and the early Christian Church.

❑ The Protestant Bible is the result of sixteenth-century reformers removing books from the Bible that didn't fit their theological agenda.

❑ In other words, Catholics use the Bible that Jesus used. Protestants use the Bible that Martin Luther thought they should use.

SEVEN

"Why Were You Baptized as a Baby?"

Most Catholics are baptized as babies — though maybe not your friend's mom who just became Catholic and was baptized at the age of 47, amazingly enough by full immersion, no less. But most of the rest of us Catholics are indeed baptized as infants.

So?

If you really must know, we're not the only Christians that practice infant baptism. Eastern Orthodox, Lutherans, Presbyterians, Methodists, and Episcopalians are a part of that big group as well.

So when your evangelical friend says Catholics aren't real Christians because we baptize babies, you might mention that he's cutting out a bunch of other people from the fold at the same time — not to speak of the vast majority of Christians who began their journeys of faith that way throughout most of history.

Once again, you should be seeing that old familiar pattern: The fundamentalist view of Christian faith and practice seems to be focused on a few elements that have absolutely nothing in common with what most Christians have believed and done through the whole existence of Christianity.

No, the majority isn't always right, and we're not appealing to that argument. But it should give you (and your friend) something to think about, anyway. If most Christians, from the earliest days of the faith, believed that infants should not be excluded from baptism, who are the modern fundamentalists to say that they should?

What's Baptism, Anyway?

The first thing you have to understand is that you, as a Catholic, and your fundamentalist friend have completely different ideas of what baptism is.

To him, baptism isn't a sacrament. His church doesn't even have sacraments. If he's Baptist, they might call baptism an "ordinance," by which they mean a ritual Jesus told His followers to perform.

But however they define it, what most evangelicals and fundamentalists hold in common is that baptism doesn't really *do* anything. You're baptized after you're "saved," after you're "born again," and baptism is a symbol of that event. It's a way of publicly showing the commitment you've made to Christ.

Now, we've talked about baptism before, and your mind should already be on red alert, after hearing what fundamentalists believe about baptism. It doesn't sound very biblical, does it?

No, it doesn't.

Let's recall what we Catholics believe about baptism, and then see whose view is better grounded in Scripture (not to mention a couple of thousand years of Christian Tradition).

Catholics believe that baptism is, of course, a sacrament. That means it's a ritual through which God really and truly acts. God shares His grace (His very life, remember?) through all of the sacraments, and baptism is no different.

Through baptism, God forgives sins (original sin and, if you're baptized as an adult, all other sins as well). We're reborn as children of God. We're joined to the new life Christ brings through His resurrection.

A good way to think about this is to see how in baptism we go down into the water, just as Jesus descended into death and into the tomb. Our old selves die there, and with Christ we rise again out of that water, reborn into that new life. Baptism also brings us into the Body of Christ – a.k.a. the Church, of course.

Now, let's see whose view is more strongly rooted in Scripture. We'll look at the meaning of baptism first.

Remember, your fundamentalist friend doesn't really believe that baptism *does* anything real. You're perfectly justified in asking him why. After all, that's not what the Bible says. Almost every time that baptism is mentioned in the New Testament, it's described as actually doing something, as a cause that brings about a definite effect.

Jesus says that we have to be born again of water and the Spirit in order to be saved (see John 3:5). In the Acts of the Apostles, when Paul relates his conversion experience, he speaks of an acquaintance telling him to "Get up and have yourself baptized and your sins washed away, calling upon his name" (Acts 22:16). In other places, Paul says that through baptism we die and rise with Christ (see Romans 6:3-4), and that we're "clothed . . . with Christ" (Galatians 3:27).

So here's your first question to the fundamentalist. (We'll get to his question in a minute – be patient. We just really believe in questioning assumptions and taking the offensive, remember?):

"Before we talk about baptizing babies, let's talk about baptism, period. Why in the world, given the evidence of Scripture (passages which you have, of course, so deftly pointed out), doesn't your church believe that baptism is vital to salvation? Why don't you believe that baptism does what the Bible says it does?"

Now for the Babies

Okay, now that you've given your friend something important to chew on, let's add to his burdens.

It's clear that his tradition's views on baptism aren't really consistent with what the Scriptures have to say about it.

So why does he believe it?

Let that simmer for a little bit, then move right on to those cute little babies, squirming under the waters of baptism.

First, ask this very simple question: "Where, in the Bible, does it prohibit infant baptism?"

(Remember, we push on this because your fundamentalist friend is particularly determined that what is in the Bible should be the only source for what Christians believe and do.)

I'll clue you in before he even has a chance to open his mouth.

Nowhere.

There's not a single line, verse, or word in the Bible that says babies shouldn't be baptized. In fact, there are hints that children younger than the age of reason were indeed baptized during apostolic times.

Jesus says, of course, to let the little children come to Him, and says it's children and those like them that will enter the kingdom of heaven (see Matthew 19:14, Mark 10:14, and Luke 18:16). He's not explicitly talking about baptism there. But if you think about His words, He doesn't seem to be saying that salvation is dependent on adult-like experiences that lead to the experience of being "born again," either.

There are, as well, several places in the New Testament in which baptism is given to entire households (Acts 16:15, Acts 16:33, and 1 Corinthians 1:16 are good places to look). No, those passages don't specifically mention children, but they don't exclude them, either. In fact, one of the stories describes Paul's jailer being baptized with all his family (see Acts 16:33).

So here's where we stand in terms of the Bible. It doesn't specifically forbid children from being baptized. A few passages imply that children might have been included in "households" or "families" that were baptized. There's not much to indicate any strong New Testament feelings either way.

It would be nice if your friend would admit this, but don't count on it.

To really get a hold on this infant-baptism stuff, though, we have to go a little bit beyond the pages of the Bible. This is going to bug your friend — and he probably won't want to do it — but it's a step you really need to take. It will help you understand the issue better, too.

Remember what I said way back when about fundamentalists being strong on Scripture (selectively, though, as you've seen) and weak on history? This is a perfect example.

We're going to look at what the early Church leaders said about baptism because we can be sure, as careful as they were to pass on the Gospel truthfully and accurately, they would certainly put a stop to any practice that the still-pretty-new Tradition passed on by the apostles seemed to prohibit.

When you look at what all of these fellows wrote about baptism, you'll find a very, very interesting thing: Not one of them condemns infant baptism.

Sure, adult baptism was the norm at the time. Why? Simply because Christianity existed in a non-Christian culture, and most people being baptized were converts from paganism and Judaism. But there were many times when, it's clear, babies were baptized, when an entire family came into Christianity.

Never, ever, is that practice condemned by these bishops who were very protective of the truth of Christianity, who were determined that the faith be preserved exactly as Jesus and the apostles taught it. If it were indeed contrary to that faith, you would think they would at least mention it, wouldn't you?

There are actually pages and pages of documentation to back this up, but I'll just cite a couple of quotes to make the point.

Irenaeus, a bishop of Lyons in the late second century, wrote:

> He [Jesus] came to save all through himself; all, I say, who through him are reborn in God – infants and children, and youths and old men. (*Against Heresies*)

During the same century, a teacher named Hippolytus, wrote instructions for baptism:

> Baptize first the children, and if they can speak for themselves, let them do so. Otherwise, let their parents or other relatives speak for them. (*The Apostolic Tradition*)

Here We Go Again!

So here we are, once again, faced with this most interesting situation.

What the "Bible-only" Christian believes about baptism doesn't seem to jibe with what the Bible says – at all.

The meaning he gives to baptism is not the meaning that the Bible gives to it.

He says babies should not be baptized. Nowhere in the Bible does it say any such thing.

He says that baptism is only for adults. Most Christians throughout history – and even present-day Christians of many denominations – don't agree. His view is an innovation in Christian thinking that's only about four hundred years old. The weight of Christian practice and

Tradition for sixteen hundred years before that had no problem with infant baptism.

The question, then, is not, "Where do Catholics get off believing that baptism has anything to do with salvation and can be given to babies?"

The question is, "Why do fundamentalists disagree with the Bible and thousands of years of Christian Tradition that reaches back to the apostles themselves?"

SO WHAT YOU SAY IS . . .

❑ Infant baptism is not prohibited by the Bible.
❑ History indicates very clearly that the tradition of infant baptism reaches back to apostolic times.
❑ Early Church leaders and teachers, who knew of the practice of infant baptism and had plenty of chances to condemn it, never condemned it. They obviously felt it was a practice consistent with the understanding of the faith that the apostles had very recently taught them.

EIGHT

"Why Aren't You Saved?"

"Have you accepted Jesus Christ as your personal Lord and Savior?"

"Are you born again?"

"Are you saved?"

"If you died tonight, are you absolutely, positively sure that you'd go to heaven?"

Sound familiar?

If you've ever had a conversation with a fundamentalist Christian about faith, I'm sure these words do indeed sound very familiar. Those deceptively simple inquiries about where you're foolish enough to think you're going to spend eternity, you silly Catholic you, are pretty basic elements of the fundamentalist repertoire.

You'll probably answer yes without much thought — but the funny thing is, you're in for it no matter what answer you give. Your yes will open you up to just as much concern as if you had admitted that you had never even heard of someone named Jesus Christ.

Here's why.

As a Catholic, when you say that, yes, you're saved; yes, you know Jesus as your Savior; and yes, you're hopeful you would go to heaven if death struck this very night, you must not expect a single word of congratulations or appreciation from your fundamentalist friend. No way. Expect, instead, even more questions.

"How do you know?"

"Are you sure you'd go to heaven? I mean, absolutely, positively sure beyond the shadow of a doubt?"

"I accepted Christ on September 7, 1994. When did you accept Him into your heart?"

Well, you'll be tempted to answer, "I love Jesus, I believe in Him, I try hard to follow Him, I receive Him in the Eucharist and try to deepen my relationship with Him all the time — and as for the date, well, there wasn't an *exact* date, unless you want to count the day I was baptized."

Baptized?

As in baptized as a *baby*?

Now you've done it. Now you've really, really done it.

For you see, to the fundamentalist Christian, *nothing* of what you've just said — not one word, believe it or not — has anything to do with your eternal salvation. If you can't point to a moment in time in which you "made a decision for Christ" in exactly the way a fundamentalist Christian thinks it should be made, you're doomed.

If this has ever happened to you, I'm sure that you feel as if you and your friend are speaking completely different languages. You're using the same words, true, but the meanings you're giving those words just aren't the same. Let's try to figure out what your friend is talking about first.

Being Saved

When fundamentalist Christians speak of "being saved," they're talking about a rather simple act, but one with eternal consequences. Sort of like the time you decided to put off writing that paper on *The Scarlet Letter* just *one more day.*

Sorry. Didn't mean to bring up unpleasant memories.

In order to understand how fundamentalist Christians believe people are saved, the first thing we have to figure out is what, exactly, they think we need to be saved *from.*

Fundamentalist Christians believe, first of all, that because of original sin, all human beings are sinners who deserve hell.

They also believe that this sin we're born with is so great, and we're so helpless in relation to God, there's nothing we ourselves can do to fix the situation.

In other words, we're doomed, and we deserve it.

All is not lost, though. Our merciful God has thrown us a life jacket through Jesus' death on the cross.

When Jesus died on the cross, He bore the punishment that human beings deserve for sin so that we don't have to bear it ourselves — if we accept it.

And once we accept it, incidentally, most fundamentalist Christians believe that salvation can *never be lost,* no matter how you live your life. I'll bet you can't wait to ask your friend her own favorite question: "And where is *that* in the Bible?" I understand, but hold off for just a minute, okay?

So "accepting Christ as your personal Savior" means that you've recognized your own wretchedness in relation to God, and that you've declared that you believe that Jesus bore the punishment you deserve.

To a fundamentalist Christian, "salvation" occurs in a moment in time in which a person just admits that she's a sinner and says that she believes that Jesus died for her sins so that she won't have to be punished for them.

What Catholics Believe

Sound nice?

Sound simple?

Simple, sure — and perhaps this thought has already crossed your mind — but is it maybe *too* simple?

Could it really be that the way you live your life has absolutely nothing to do with salvation?

And hey — what about baptism? The Bible — Jesus Himself, you're almost sure — says a lot about baptism and salvation. Why doesn't that little detail come into your friend's explanation of how to get saved?

You are, I have to admit, just too smart.

You've just about figured it all out already. Let me help you finish it off.

Catholics agree with fundamentalist Christians on a lot of points here:

- We agree that sin separates us from God.
- We agree that without God's grace, we're doomed.
- We agree that Jesus redeemed us by His life, death, and resurrection.
- We agree that faith in Christ and the freely given grace of God are what save us.

But beyond that, there are huge differences. The funny thing is that, in reality, the Catholic view of salvation is, ironically enough, much more biblically-based than the fundamentalist view. In fact, the only way that a fundamentalist can defend her opinions on salvation is to flat-out ignore a lot of what the Bible says about it. But we're not going to ignore them here.

The easiest way to see the difference between the Catholic and evangelical viewpoints on salvation is this: Evangelical and fundamentalist Christians see salvation as a *moment*. Catholics understand salvation as a *process*.

So how are we saved?

Evangelicals would say that human salvation begins with Jesus' death. The effects of that death come to a person when she accepts Christ as her Savior.

Catholics believe that the gifts of forgiveness and justification which Jesus' death brings to human beings are given to a person when she is baptized. In baptism, she is given grace — God's life within her very soul.

But that, of course, is only the beginning.

As we grow in age, we also grow with Christ. Every moment of every day, God continues to offer us His life — grace. Through that grace, He helps us respond to life in ways that bring us closer to Him and even make us more like Him, day by day.

We can call this process "sanctification," or "growing in holiness."

That's the difference between the Catholic and the fundamentalist views: We believe that Jesus' saving act does indeed make things right in the universe and in our souls. But if we don't cooperate with that freely given grace, we're not holy, we're not regenerated, we're not any closer to being in God's image than we were before we knew about that act of salvation.

On the other hand, if we do cooperate with God's love and grace, then at the end of our lives we'll stand before Him with our whole lives (not just one moment), lives that we've opened to Him (not lives hidden from Him), lives that reflect His light (not lives that simply shut it out). That's salvation.

> **Lord my God, you have formed and reformed me.**
>
> St. Anselm,
> *Prayer of St. Anselm*

Why Do We Believe What We Believe?

There's no doubt that by this time, your fundamentalist friend is going to have a lot to say. Tempers might even be flaring a bit, to tell the truth. But you really have to forge on, and remember a few points.

Do not – at any time, and especially now – allow your friend to tell you what the Catholic Church teaches. She's prone to throw out all kinds of simplistic, misleading characterizations of Catholic teaching that she's heard from her own church, and which are simply not true.

When you talk about what the Catholic Church has taught about salvation for two thousand years, talk about the truth. Use what I'm telling you in this book. Go straight to the source – The *Catechism of the Catholic Church* – and quote from that. Don't be swayed by fundamentalist caricatures of our Church's teaching. Stick to your guns, be firm, and just keep patiently correcting.

And then, having handled that former problem with ease, move right on to your friend's favorite spot: the Bible.

You might want to ask, before you really get into the Catholic view, why your friend believes what she does about that moment of "being saved." Where, exactly in Scripture, does anyone — Jesus, Paul, or whoever — say that a person's salvation revolves around that very specific act of being "born again" in the *particular way she's talking about it?*

She'll have some passages to share with you, to be sure. Go ahead and read them with her, but with a completely open mind. Sure, the passages she'll cite speak of faith in Christ as what brings us salvation. They'll speak of that salvation being undeserved and a free gift from God.

But — if you read them without prejudice or an agenda — do they actually mean what she claims they do? Is she really reading them as they "literally" are (here we are, back to that again!), or is she interpreting them according to what her church has told her they should or even must mean?

Now it's your turn: time for you to go on the offensive, and to trot out all the very handy Bible passages that are at the root of the Catholic teaching on salvation. The best way to do this is just give you a list and let you go at it:

Justification has *been merited for us by the Passion of Christ* who offered himself on the cross has a living victim, holy and pleasing to God, and whose blood has become the instrument of atonement for the sins of all men.

Catechism of the Catholic Church **(No. 1992)**

Salvation Is a Process

- *So then, my beloved, obedient as you have always been . . . work out your salvation with fear and trembling.* (Philippians 2:12)

- *Brothers, I for my part do not consider myself to have taken possession. Just one thing: forgetting what lies behind but straining forward to what lies ahead, I continue my pursuit toward the goal, the prize of God's upward calling, in Christ Jesus.* (PHILIPPIANS 3:13-14)
- *If we have died with him, we shall also live with him; if we persevere we shall also reign with him.* (2 TIMOTHY 2:11-12)

You see a trend, don't you? These Scripture passages definitely point to salvation as a process that's not over until we have left this life, and not a moment before. How does your fundamentalist friend make sense of the plain meaning of these verses and still say that we're saved in one moment, and that after that moment our salvation can never be lost?

Salvation Begins With Baptism

- *Jesus answered, "Amen, amen, I say to you, no one can enter the kingdom of God without being born of water and Spirit."* (JOHN 3:5)
- *Are you unaware that we who were baptized into Christ Jesus were baptized into his death? We were indeed buried with him through baptism into death, so that, just as Christ was raised from the dead by the glory of the Father, we too might live in newness of life.* (ROMANS 6:3-4)

We're going to talk about baptism more specifically in an upcoming chapter, but it's important for you to see those passages now. They point out that from New Testament times, Christians have seen the process of salvation as being tied very closely to the grace we receive in the waters of baptism.

So Who's "Bible-based" Now?

Here's the point we're trying to make about this very complicated matter called salvation: There is hardly a scrap of evidence in either the Bible — honestly read — or in most of the history of Christianity to support the fundamentalists' claim of what salvation is all about.

They'll claim that it comes in a single moment of decision.

The Scriptures don't have any passages supporting that and, in fact, frequently speak of salvation as a process that begins with the grace God gives through the waters of baptism.

They'll say that the sinner isn't really changed by accepting Christ, that he remains a sinner.

The Scriptures and Christian Tradition clearly say, over and over, that in this process of salvation our goal is indeed to cooperate with God's grace, to change, to grow in holiness, and to become more Christ-like every day.

So what you should clearly see, and be confident in saying, is that there doesn't seem to be much evidence in Scripture to support your Bible-only friend's notion of salvation. The evidence really points the other way.

Like so many conversations you'll have with your friend, your ability to discuss this without getting completely confused depends on how clearly you see that the fundamentalist perspective is, quite frankly, wrong. You can't accept their assumptions. No, the Catholic Church doesn't speak of 'being saved" and "born again" in the same way your friend's church does.

But — and please get this through your head — perhaps that's because the particular points that the fundamentalist makes about salvation are wrong! And that simple fact makes it a lot easier to answer that question of whether you're saved or not. Here's how one useful apologetics source suggests you answer the question, "Are you saved?":

> "As the Bible says, I am already saved (Rom. 8:24, Eph. 2:5-8), but I'm also *being* saved (1 Cor. 1:8, 2 Cor. 2:15, Phil. 2:12), and I have the hope that I *will be* saved (Rom. 5:9-10, 1 Cor. 3:12-15). I am redeemed . . . and like the Apostle Paul I am working out my salvation in fear and trembling (Phil. 2:12), with hopeful confidence in the promises of Christ (Rom. 5:2, 2 Tim. 2:11-13) — but not with a false 'absolute' assurance about my own ability to persevere (2 Cor. 13:5). And I do all this as the Catholic Church has taught, unchanged, from the time of Christ." (Catholic Answers tract "No 'Assurance of Salvation' ")

SO WHAT YOU SAY IS . . .

❑ The Catholic view of salvation is rooted in what the Bible says about it.
❑ The New Testament tells us that salvation comes through the sacrifice of Jesus on the cross.
❑ The New Testament makes it very clear that the saving effects of that sacrifice come to us through baptism.

❑ The New Testament tells us that when we live a life in cooperation with the grace of God, we grow in holiness. The end of this journey lies with God in heaven. We trust in the promise, but we're not presumptuous about it, either. As the Bible indicates, when a Christian sins, he puts his salvation at risk.

❑ There's no biblical evidence for the fundamentalist Christian beliefs that salvation is wrapped up in a single moment of assent; or that the conduct of our lives has nothing to do with salvation; or that salvation, once "accepted," can never be lost.

NINE

"Why Does Your Church Say You're Saved by Works, Not by Faith?"

Once again, you find yourself stumped and puzzled.

In the middle of one of your usually fun-filled faith conversations, your fundamentalist friend has started talking a foreign language again. And more importantly, she's started telling you, once more, what the Catholic Church teaches. You're bemused and skeptical. You should be.

With this topic, we've entered into the second big area of dispute between traditional Reformation Protestantism and the two-thousand-year-old Tradition of the Catholic Church. (In case you've forgotten, the first was the dispute over Scripture and Tradition.)

Faith and Works

Your friend has started on this big speech in which she's telling you that Catholics believe that human beings are saved by their own efforts — how many prayers they say, whether they go to Mass every Sunday, and what kind of charity they engage in. In other words, she says that you, as a Catholic, believe that you get to heaven because of your "works."

On the other hand, she says — with one hand on the Bible, of course — that her church teaches the correct idea, the one that's taught by Jesus and Paul, the one that's in the Bible: Your efforts have absolutely nothing to do with your salvation. You're saved by God's grace alone. You can't earn your way to heaven.

She's done it again, hasn't she?

She's sown the seeds of doubt once more. She's recited a bunch of Bible passages that seem to support the fundamentalist view, leaving you wondering.

If the Catholic Church really does teach that we're saved by works and not by God's freely given grace, and if the Bible supports the latter view (as her unending stream of verses seem to indicate it does), could it be that what the Church teaches is wrong?

Could it be — gulp — that by teaching this unbiblical doctrine, the Catholic Church has misled you and taught

you a way of faith that is going to get you the exact opposite of salvation?

I really wish you would stop letting your friend do this
to you.

Haven't you learned anything yet?

Haven't you discerned a pattern yet?

Can't you already see what's coming?

Once again, we're going to get at the truth, and we're
going to see that, first, her characterization of Catholic teaching is just too wrong for words and, second, that her fundamentalist views on this matter, like everything else we've
covered, are not, as she claims, biblically-based at all. In fact,
the only way her tradition can maintain its views on this
issue is by ignoring some pretty important parts of the Bible.

Let's get to it.

Where It All Comes From

If you've studied the Protestant Reformation, you have
a general idea of what this whole "Faith vs. Works" contro-
versy was and is still all about. It's all about our old friend
Martin Luther.

As you probably remember, Martin Luther was a Catholic monk and professor of Scripture who lived in sixteenth-
century Germany. Luther was very serious about his faith,
but he had one little problem, and that problem actually
has a name. We call it "scrupulosity."

You see, Martin Luther, quite unfortunately, could not
feel the love and forgiveness of God in his soul. No matter
what he did — no matter how many times he went to confession (several times a week!), no matter how much he
prayed — he still felt like an incredible sinner.

He did every religious practice known to the sixteenth-century German Catholic, but none of it helped. He lived his days under a cloud of condemnation, fearful of God's wrath, and never feeling any comfort in his faith.

Then one day, deep in the midst of despair, Luther read a Scripture passage. It was a verse from Paul's Letter to the Romans:

> For in it is revealed the righteousness of God from faith to faith; as it is written, "The one who is righteous by faith will live." (1:17)

In this moment, Luther realized something that changed not only his life, but also the entire history of the world.

There was, indeed, nothing he could do to "earn" God's forgiveness. God's forgiveness is freely given, even though it's undeserved. Like the father of the prodigal son, God offers us His love unconditionally, simply because He is Love.

Very soon after that, Luther began to look around him at the religious practices of his culture, and what he saw disturbed him. He saw that a lot of the popular beliefs and practices of his fellow Catholics seemed to revolve around the hope that they could indeed "earn" grace. Some practices gave the impression that grace could even be bought for a few coins donated to your favorite shrine or religious cause. And so, "Faith vs. Works" was born.

In the historical context, and given Luther's personal obsession, you can see how such a reaction would very easily set in.

The problem, of course, is that while Catholic popular religious practice may have taken an unfortunate turn that tended to lead people to believe that their works were more important than God's grace when it came to salvation, that wasn't what the Catholic Church was really teaching at the time. In fact, it had never taught any such thing at all.

You're wondering how that can happen — such a dissonance between Church teaching and popular practice. You're wondering if that isn't just a cop-out. Well, just consider this. Think today about how many teachings of the Catholic Church are ignored by people who call themselves Catholic: the sanctity of life, the priority that caring for the poor should have in our own lives, and the vital importance of attending and participating in Mass every single Sunday. Do you see where we're going?

And what your fundamentalist friend is talking about right now is what the Catholic Church teaches about salvation — not how that teaching could potentially be misunderstood.

So is she right?

Of Course Not!

And at the risk of being rude, we might add, has she been right about *anything* she claimed the Catholic Church teaches? No? Then what are you so worried about?

Remember, we're dealing with reality here, not fundamentalist fantasies about Catholicism. So, let's go right to the source — that Big Book that comes from Rome, written by the People Who Should Know in the Vatican, that official book we (and everyone else) call the *Catechism of the Catholic Church*:

> Since the initiative belongs to God in the order of grace, *no one can merit the initial grace* of forgiveness

and justification, at the beginning of conversion. (No.
2010)

Our justification comes from the grace of God. Grace
is *favor*, the *free and undeserved help* that God gives us
to respond to his call to become children of God, adop-
tive sons, partakers of the divine nature and of eternal
life. (No. 1996)

Can we make it any clearer?

The Catholic Church obviously teaches that we're saved
because God chooses to save us. His grace is freely given,
undeserved, and shared with us through the sacrifice of
Jesus on the cross.

Now here's where the difference comes, and it's an important one. And you'll be pleased to know that the biblical
evidence is *totally* supportive of the Catholic view of this
difference.

But . . . Faith Alone?

Your fundamentalist friend, like her faraway ancestor in
faith, Martin Luther, is going to maintain that we're saved
not only by our faith, but also by faith alone. She's going to
say that our "works" have nothing to do with that salvation.

And like Martin Luther, the only way she's going to be
able to hold to this distinctly unhistorical and unbiblical
view is by selective reading of the Bible. For you see, the
Catholic Church teaches that, yes, we are saved by grace
alone, but we're not saved by faith alone.

Ah ha! Do you see now? No? Okay, let's try again.

God's grace is the beginning and the end of our salvation — we talked about that in the last chapter. His grace is

showered on us through the sacrifice of Jesus through baptism. When we cooperate with that grace, we're strengthened to grow in holiness and become more like that Divine Image. That holiness — and here's the important part — involves beliefs *and* actions both. But — listen hard now — *all of it – even the good works that we do –* are only possible because of God's grace.

Here's a good quote from Paul to explain what we mean:

> *But by the grace of God I am what I am, and his grace to me has not been ineffective. Indeed, I have toiled harder than all of them; not I, however, but the grace of God [that is] with me.* (1 CORINTHIANS 15:10)

So, yes, God's grace is responsible for our salvation. But is our faith in that grace *all that is needed* for salvation?

Well, your friend would say yes — that goes back to the whole "born again" and "accepting Christ" idea that we dissected in the last chapter. So you know she's going to say yes.

But sadly, and oh so tragically, that's not what the Bible says. Not at all.

Faith Without Works Is . . . DEAD!

Martin Luther was a funny guy. He was smart, certainly, and he had some important concerns about Church life that were ultimately addressed when the Church engaged in a vigorous effort to reform itself and clean up abuses later in the sixteenth century. But the thing is, Martin Luther wasn't above manipulating Scripture to emphasize his points.

Let's take the Letter of James, a particularly annoying thorn in Martin Luther's side, to show how this worked.

If you read the Letter of James, you'll see that it's a work that really emphasizes the importance of – well, to put it bluntly – works. In fact, there's a verse in it that says quite explicitly

> *See how a person is justified by works and not by faith alone. . . . [F]aith without works is dead.* (2:24, 26)

So how did Martin Luther deal with this very strong evidence from the Bible that this rather important element of his theology was wrong? Easy. Ditch it. As in ditch the whole book. (Other Reformers were, of course, uncomfortable with this idea, so today the Protestant Bible includes James. But if Martin Luther had had his way, it wouldn't be. Talk about a "man-made" faith!)

No, your fundamentalist friend might be distressed to hear you say that there's really nowhere in the Bible that justifies anyone teaching that our actions are irrelevant to salvation.

> **God works in man many good things to which man does not contribute; but man does not work any good things apart from God, since it is from God man receives the power to do the good things he does.**
>
> St. Augustine of Hippo,
> *Two Letters Against the Pelagians*

But let's make an important distinction one more time.

The good works that we do don't "earn" our way into heaven. They make us holier, they bring us closer to God, and they are evidence that faith is alive and well in our souls. Further, the good works aren't due to our own fabulousness. They are totally rooted in God's grace, working within us.

But, as the whole Bible teaches, those good works, done under the power of God's grace, are important in salvation. Here are a few verses (besides James, of course!) to help you out:

> *"Not everyone who says to me, 'Lord, Lord,' will enter the kingdom of heaven, but only the one who does the will of my Father in heaven.* (MATTHEW 7:21)

> *The one who sows for his flesh will reap corruption from the flesh, but the one who sows for the spirit will reap eternal life from the spirit. Let us not grow tired of doing good, for in due time we shall reap our harvest, if we do not give up.* (GALATIANS 6:8-9)

> *I saw the dead, the great and the lowly, standing before the throne, and scrolls were opened. Then another scroll was opened, the book of life. The dead were judged according to their deeds, by what was written in the scrolls.* (REVELATION 20:12)

And don't forget to ask your friend to explain exactly what Matthew 25:14-46 means if indeed our actions have nothing to do with salvation. I'll let you discover what those passages are all about on your own.

A Word About Paul and the Law

A lot — and I mean *a lot* — of your friend's evidence for the fundamentalist position is going to come from a couple of Paul's letters in particular: his Letter to the Romans (especially Chapters 2 through 8) and the Letter to the Galatians (particularly Chapters 2 through 4).

If you take a quick look at these passages, you might think, *Hey! This is all about being saved by faith, not by works or the Law! Doesn't this support the fundamentalist view?*

Not at all. If your friend starts to rely on these passages, take a break of a day or two. Go home, read them over yourself (from your *Catholic* Bible, remember?), and remember the following context as you read.

In both letters, Paul was, at least in part, addressing Christians who had converted from Judaism. In many cases, they still engaged in a lot of Jewish practices — it wasn't until the end of the first century that Judaism and Christianity completely separated.

It was one of the huge conflicts of early Christianity: Did you have to be Jewish in order to be Christian? Did even former pagans who became Christian have to observe the Jewish Law? Did Christians need to observe the Jewish dietary laws, and did Christian men need to be circumcised?

> **The law detects, [but] grace alone conquers sin.**
>
> St. Augustine of Hippo

After much prayer and reflection, Paul, a former rabbi himself, came to the conclusion that they didn't. In these letters, he explains why, often to people who are being tempted by teachers and preachers who believe the opposite, who were coming into Christian communities declaring, "Ah! You're not observing the Law! Then you're not Christian, either!"

So you simply must see Paul's words about faith, the Law, and "works" in that context. He wasn't speaking in general terms about the good that we do, empowered by God's grace. He was talking about the specifics of the Jew-

ish Law. His basic point was this: The Jewish Law had
served its purpose. Now that Jesus had come, it wasn't
necessary.

Notice — he is quite specifically talking about the Jewish Law. In this context, every single word Paul says about
"works" is in relation to the Jewish Law, not to doing good
in general.

How do we know this?

Because in so many other places, (as in the verses we
cited above), Paul indicates the importance of our actions
to salvation.

Here's Where You Stand

The Catholic Church teaches that salvation comes
through the grace of God. It's the grace of God alone that
brings the possibility of salvation into our world and into
our individual lives.

Faith — that is, trust in the promises of Christ and God's
forgiveness — plays a vital role in our salvation. But not
the only role.

Scripture and Christian Tradition make it very clear that
what we do in relation to God's freely given grace plays a
role in our final salvation.

The question then, very neatly turned around is this,
and I really hope you ask it: Given the evidence of Scripture, how in the world can your evangelical friend say that
our actions have no impact on our salvation?

After all, that's not what the Bible says about it.

SO WHAT YOU SAY IS . . .

- ❑ Catholics believe that salvation comes through acceptance of and cooperation with God's freely given grace: That's faith.
- ❑ Catholics believe that what Jesus told us is true: Our actions affect our salvation.
- ❑ Catholics believe that the good that we do is important in regard to our salvation. But we also believe that our "power" to do good has nothing to do with us, and everything to do with God.
- ❑ There's simply no support for the fundamentalist view of faith and works in the Scriptures. Jesus and Paul both indicate that we'll be judged, in part, by our earthly actions. And when Paul speaks of obedience to the Law as being powerless to save, he's talking to Jewish Christians about the replacement of the Old Covenant with the New Covenant through Jesus.

TEN

"Why Do You Pray to Saints?"

You may be startled by this question, and, depending on your background, you'll be startled for one of two reasons.

First, you may be a person who's grown up in a household and family in which praying to saints is as natural as calling up Grandma on Saturday morning. You may know everything there is to know about your own patron saint, and maybe you've even got a good St. Anthony story to tell, like this little rhyme:

> Tony, Tony, come around,
> Something's lost and must be found!

So being asked why you pray to saints is about as strange a question as being asked why you eat breakfast. You just do, that's all — and you always have.

Or you could be a person who's never prayed to a saint at all. You're Catholic, sure, but devotion to saints just hasn't been a part of your life so far.

If that's you, the question's going to come as a surprise — not only because you can't answer it, but because you're going to be puzzled by it yourself. *Hey*, you'll find yourself thinking, *why do we pray to saints, anyway?*

Why and . . . Why Not?

First of all, let's make sure everyone understands what a saint is.

The *Catechism of the Catholic Church* says that saints are people who "practiced heroic virtue and lived in fidelity to God's grace" (no. 828).

The Church formally recognizes some of the many who have lived this way — that process is called "canonization" — but canonized saints certainly are not the only people who have lived this way through history, and the Church knows this. That's part of the reason why we have that feast day on November 1 called All Saints' Day — to offer thanksgiving to God for *all* the saints, whether they are formally recognized or not.

By the way, it's good for you to know that Catholics aren't the only folks who venerate saints. The Eastern Orthodox and Anglicans (or Episcopalians, as most of them are known in the United States) do as well, and you'll even find Presbyterian, Lutheran, and Methodist churches scattered here and there named after saints.

> **To most, even good people, God is a belief. To the saints He is an embrace.**
>
> FRANCIS THOMPSON,
> *Works,* Vol. III

"Well," your friend might say, "it's fine to talk about people who've been close friends with God and can be role models for us, but why pray to them? Surely you know that we're only supposed to worship God alone. Why do you Catholics pray to anyone else but the one God?"

Okay, here's where you have to tease apart some definitions.

Catholics believe — along with every other Christian, Jew, and Muslim on the planet — that prayer *as worship* is something we give to God alone. That's what the First Commandment is all about, and we obey it.

But our prayer to saints is not — most definitely *not* — worship. When we pray to saints, we're not honoring them as Creator of the universe, as the One who gives us life and every other good thing. We're not asking them to forgive our sins or thanking them for the grace and gift of salvation. That would not only be wrong; it would pretty dumb and useless, too.

That's all worship, and that belongs to God.

No, when we pray to saints, we're doing something quite different: We're asking them to pray for us. Period.

In fact, *to pray* originally meant "to ask," when it first emerged in the English language. You might have encountered this usage of it in medieval and Early Renaissance writing in places where people say things like, "I pray thee, please don't chop off my fingers, my Lord." It was only after the Reformation that the phrase *to pray* was narrowed down to mean words directed to God, mostly in the Protestant, English-speaking world.

In the Catholic world, *pray* still held that broader meaning — it can mean worship, but it can also refer to the words we use when we're talking to our friends in heaven (the saints).

Once again, we're going to be back in a place in which your fundamentalist friend is undoubtedly going to try to instruct you about what the Catholic Church is all about. Don't let him. You insist on doing the instructing — after all, you're the Catholic, aren't you?

Just keep reminding your friend of the truth, that Catholic devotion to saints involves one of three things: asking the saints to pray for us; praying prayers to God that the saints wrote themselves; or offering thanks to God for the good example and holiness of the saints.

Not a bit of worship involved.

Now, your friend is going to say, "But why pray to saints, when you can pray to God directly?" And even more importantly, he'll say, "You don't need all those saints to pray for you. Jesus is the one mediator (go-between) between us and God the Father. Why put all these other people in the way?"

Good question.

As we find is so often true, right here and now, we'll answer that question with yet another question.

Simply ask this of your friend: "In your church, do people ever pray for each other? Do members of your church pray for those who are sick? Do they pray for members of the church who are having family problems? Do they pray for the lost to come to Christ? Do they pray for the hungry and oppressed throughout the world?"

Of course they do.

You know where this is going, don't you?

It's time for you to ask your friend, "Why? Why do you ask other people to pray for you? Why not just pray to God yourself? Hmmm?"

What your friend needs to understand is that for Catholics, our Church doesn't just exist in the present. Our family of faith isn't defined only by those who happen to be alive on earth right this minute.

We believe that the holy ones are, of course, alive right now and live forever with God. We call that the "Communion of Saints."

So, just as members of their church pray for one another, members of our Church pray for each other, too — *all* of our Church's members: those with us now on earth, and those with God in heaven.

If you believe in the power of prayer, and if you believe in eternal life, why not ask those in heaven to pray for you?

Finally, some Scripture passages are in order here, to help your friend see that all of this has a good basis in the Bible.

First of all, there are lots of places in the New Testament that tell us it's a good thing to pray for each other:

> *You help us with prayer, so that thanks may be given by many on our behalf for the gift granted us through the prayers of many."* (2 CORINTHIANS 1:11).

> *Finally, brothers, pray for us, so that the word of the Lord may speed forward and be glorified, as it did among you, and that we may be delivered from perverse and wicked people, for not all have faith"* (2 THESSALONIANS 3:1-2).

Now, gently make that leap.

The Bible tells us over and over that it's a good thing for people to pray for one another. Where in the Bible does it say the deceased are excluded from that circle?

Might it even be that there's a place or two in the Bible that seemingly *includes* them? Let's look:

> *When he took [the scroll], the four living creatures and the twenty-four elders fell down before the Lamb. Each of the elders held a harp and gold bowls filled with incense, which are the prayers of the holy ones.* (REVELATION 5:8).

Remember, all the scenes in Revelation are parts of a vision that the author John had of what was going on in heaven. What he describes here are people and creatures in heaven offering the prayers of people on earth (referred to here as "the holy ones") to God. They're praying to God on behalf of people on earth.

It's clear now why Catholics pray to saints. We hope and trust that these holy people will pray for us.

And considering how tough life can be, why would anyone *not* want to ask for saints' prayers as we make that journey?

SO WHAT YOU SAY IS . . .

- ❑ All Christians pray for one another, all the time.
- ❑ The Bible encourages us to pray for one another.
- ❑ Catholics believe that people in heaven can pray for us just as well as people on earth can.
- ❑ Saints are important to Catholics for just that reason: They're holy people whose lives give us wonderful role models in faith, and who can pray for us. Period.

ELEVEN

"Why Do You Honor
Mary So Much?"

To fundamentalist Christians, Mary sits right up there with the pope and purgatory on the "List of the Top Three Reasons We Seriously Doubt Catholics Are Really Christians."

Our veneration of Mary bugs them no end. Why? Because to the fundamentalist, the role of Mary in the Catholic faith expresses the single worst aspect of Catholicism: finding religious truth outside the Bible.

The absolute first thing you're going to have to clear up is the misconception that Catholics "worship" Mary. We don't. We honor her. Why shouldn't we?

After all, you should point out to your friend, Mary was kind of important in the history of salvation. Her "yes" to God cleared the way for Jesus to enter the world. She was, if you think about it, the first disciple, faithful to Jesus even at the foot of the cross, a spot that was conspicuously deserted by all of the apostles except for John.

Why not honor her?

Our attitude toward Mary is rooted in the same perspective we bring to the saints: Since we honor people who achieve worldly success, then why not honor, remember, study, and try to emulate people in our history who have been particularly holy, Mary included?

If your friend is going to ignorantly insist that Catholics "worship" Mary, all you really need to do is this: Go over the most common prayer directed at Mary. We call it the "Hail Mary," of course:

Hail Mary, full of grace,
the Lord is with you.
blessed are you among women,
and blessed is the fruit of your womb, Jesus.
Holy Mary, Mother of God,
pray for us sinners,
now and at the hour of our death.
Amen.

Invite your friend to ponder these words, then get out your Bible. (You didn't forget it did you?)

Go over the first part of that prayer, and point out that every word is derived, not from any "man-made" tradition, but from the Bible itself. The first two lines are part of what the angel said to Mary at the event we call the "Annunciation" (see Luke 1:28). If your friend quibbles on the translation of "full of grace" in the prayer, which is a little different from modern Scripture versions that translate the Greek into "most favored one," please point out that the Greek word used here means a lot more than "to be happy with" — it means the person has received God's blessings in their fullness.

The next two lines come from the Bible, too — from the words Elizabeth says to her cousin Mary at the Visitation, recorded in Luke 1:42.

So there you have it. Half of this prayer that fundamentalists think is so awful actually comes right from the Bible, and the other half is simply a request for Mary to pray for us.

Can you help wondering what the big deal is? Isn't it odd that your "Bible-only" friend has such a big objection to Catholics praying with words taken directly from the Bible?

Those Difficult Beliefs

That wasn't too hard, was it?

You've made it very clear that Catholics absolutely do not worship Mary, and that the prayers we say to her, like those we direct to any saint, are mostly asking her to pray for us, just as you hope your own mom and grandmother are praying for you!

But what about those funny beliefs we have? For you know, your friend has already started mentioning them — the Immaculate Conception, the Assumption, and Mary's perpetual virginity.

He's hooked on these teachings as sure evidence that Catholicism isn't about a Bible-based faith, but about something else instead.

We're going to look at these teachings very briefly — and as we do, it's very important that you remember this: No, these teachings are *not* explicitly mentioned in the Bible. But all of them are rooted in hints God has given us in Scripture, none of them are anti-biblical, and every one of them has been a part of Christian Tradition almost since the beginning.

Let's take them one at a time.

The Immaculate Conception

The Immaculate Conception (celebrated on December 8) is one of the more widely misunderstood Catholic teachings, maybe even by you.

This concept *does not* (Did you hear me? *Does not!*) refer to Jesus' being conceived without help of a human father — that's called the Virginal Conception of Christ.

No, this teaching simply means that Mary was conceived without original sin.

Now, I predict, your fundamentalist friend is going to jump on this with a rather bizarre level of enthusiasm: "Where is that in the Bible? Doesn't that make Mary the equivalent of Jesus?" And again: "Where is that in the Bible?"

Yawn.

Here's what you say:

- Our first hint lies in those words of the angel to Mary: "full of grace." We explained before how this means that Mary was the recipient of the fullness of God's blessing.
- Secondly, it's clear, logically speaking, that if Mary was to be the mother of Jesus — the one true God — she would need to be a worthy vessel. That is, free from the stain of sin. Doesn't that make sense?
- So, our faith teaches us, God took care of that little detail. God, who has the power to save all of us from sin, and whose grace makes us holy and blameless in His sight, did this for Mary, too. It's just that He worked this moment and process of grace long before the gift came to the rest of us — at her conception, freeing her from original sin. He did this, not for her sake, but for ours.

And did you get the full implication of that last point? Mary being "full of grace" and free from original sin has nothing to do with her own merits, and everything to do with God's grace. She didn't do it. God freed her from sin, just as He makes His saving grace available to all of us.

It's possible that your friend is going to whip out a verse or two in defense of his position that the Mother of God was infected by sin — something like Romans 3:23: "All have sinned and are deprived of the glory of God." Here's how to answer that one.

First, what does it mean? Does it mean that we're all part of the human race, which falls under the tragedy of original sin?

If so, well then, sure, Mary falls under that category — but God saved her from it, and early, too, so she would be ready to receive and bear Jesus.

But if your friend insists that this verse means that every single person has actually sinned (a far less likely interpretation), is that really true? What about babies and very young children? Have they sinned? Oh, we see an exception here. Could it be that perhaps Paul was trying to make another point? Read the entire part of that chapter.

It's clear that in this context, Paul is talking about the relative status of Jews and pagans in relation to God. He's saying that both stand in equal need of Jesus' salvation, that neither group is more privileged than the other.

I'm telling you, it's really important to stop your fundamentalist friend every single time he throws a Scripture verse at you. Nine times out of ten, you'll find that the verse, when taken in context, has absolutely nothing to do with the point he's attempting to prove.

It's sort of like situations in which a movie critic will say that "This film was an amazing piece of trash. It's unbelievable that any moviegoer would be crazy enough to pay

to go see it" — words that, on the movie poster, are strangely transformed into a positive review: . . . Amazing! . . . Unbelievable! . . . Crazy! . . . Go see it!" Yup. It's just like that.

So don't buy the nonsense that Catholics see Mary as some sort of goddess with powers of her own. It's just not true. Mary was a human being like the rest of us, saved by God's grace for His own loving purpose!

The Assumption

This one follows closely on the Immaculate Conception.

The Bible teaches us that one of the consequences of sin was death (go check out Genesis 3 to see how this works). It makes sense that if Mary was preserved from original sin, then God preserved her from the corruption of physical death as well.

And your friend needs to know that this is not exactly an unknown phenomenon in Scripture. For example, in

2 Kings 2:11, it's reported that Elijah, instead of dying, was taken up into heaven in a fiery chariot.

If God could do this for Elijah, why not Mary?

Another interesting point to make to your friend is that the early Christians took very good care of the remains and tombs of those who had died, especially the giants of the faith. The Mediterranean area, from Egypt all the way around up through Spain, is filled with historical and ar- cheological sites that have long histories of being associ- ated with the tombs of lots of early saints and holy people.

But not Mary. There's not one site anywhere in Pales- tine or thereabouts that has ever, through history, claimed to be Mary's *final* resting place. Isn't that curious? (Dormition Abbey on Mount Zion, in Jerusalem, is the place where, it is said, Mary "fell asleep in the Lord." But there is, of course, no tomb containing her body.)

So all of that leads us to this ancient belief of Christians: When Mary's life on earth was finished, she was taken up (*assumed*) body and soul into heaven — hence, the feast of the Assumption, celebrated in our churches on August 15.

By the way, the importance of both of these teachings doesn't just lie in what they say about Mary. They also say important things about us: that God has the power to save us from sin; and that, when all is said and done, He'll bring our whole selves — souls and glorified bodies — to be with Him forever in heaven!

Mary's Perpetual Virginity

This, you'll find, is a big one, although it really doesn't have the same implications that the other two teachings have. But fundamentalist Christians love to talk about it because, once again, it casts doubt on how seriously Catholics take Scripture.

For you see, there are, indeed, several places in Scripture in which Jesus' "brothers and sisters" are referred to, and one of the early Church leaders was widely known as "James, the brother of the Lord."

So why, the fundamentalist wonders, do Catholics (once again!) fly in the face of the plain meaning of Scripture and insist that Jesus didn't have any blood brothers or sisters and that Mary remained a virgin her entire life?

Here's why. (This is kind of technical, but there's no other way to explain it. It's kind of interesting too, though.) Those who translated the Gospels into Greek, long ago, were working out of two other languages: Hebrew and Aramaic — the language of the Old Testament and the common spoken language of Jesus' time, respectively.

Neither Hebrew nor Aramaic has any word that specifically means "cousin" or "nephew." The only word they had to refer to any male relative was "brother."

There are lots of places in the Old Testament that make this clear. Here are a few of them:

- Genesis 14:14 refers to Lot as Abraham's brother, but he was really his nephew.
- In Genesis 29:15, Laban's nephew Jacob is called his brother.
- In Deuteronomy 23:7 and Jeremiah 34:9, the word "brother" is used to refer to just kinsmen in general.

So this is what happened. When the writers of the New Testament books (which were, we think, originally written in Greek) were pulling all of their resources together to tell the story of Jesus, most of the stories they had heard had come down to them in either Hebrew or Aramaic. All of the references to Jesus' "brothers" that his Aramaic-speaking apostles had made and passed down were very simply translated into Greek, without really bothering to pick apart whether those relations were cousins, uncles, or real blood brothers at all.

Another good point to make is that there is a very important moment in which you would think any real brothers and sisters of Jesus would be mentioned: that moment on the cross when Jesus gave Mary into the care of His apostle John.

The implication is clear that after His death, Mary would be alone, with no one to take care of her. If Jesus did have real blood brothers and sisters, why did He need John to care for His mother?

Back to History

Here we are, back again, at the fundamentalist Christian's least favorite spot: history.

Actually, he might bring up a couple of points of history himself, and you need to be ready for them.

He'll remind you (or tell you, in case you didn't already know) that the doctrine of the Immaculate Conception wasn't officially defined by the Church until 1854, and the Assumption not until 1950.

Upon delivering these bits of news, he'll sit back, triumphant, with that "Gotcha!" look on his face, I've no doubt.

Well, he doesn't gotcha. Not at all. He just doesn't understand how the Catholic Church works.

The Catholic Church, contrary to popular fundamentalist belief, does not live and die by official pronouncements. We know that Sacred Tradition is a river that runs wide and deep, all the way back to Jesus and the apostles, across every age and culture.

There have been lots of Catholic teachings that were believed for centuries before they were officially "defined." The Immaculate Conception and the Assumption are two of them.

In fact, all three of these beliefs about Mary were held by Christians from the first century onward — we have evidence from the writings of the early Church Fathers for that. These were items of faith that were simply taken for granted as true, and this was the case for centuries.

As a matter of fact, it might be very interesting for your friend to hear that the very first official Protestant, Martin Luther, believed in the Immaculate Conception *and* the Assumption of Mary. In addition, *all* of the early Protestant Reformers, from Luther to John Calvin (Presbyterian churches trace their origins back to Calvin, by the way), also believed in the perpetual virginity of Mary — that Jesus had no blood brothers or sisters. Your fundamentalist friend's beliefs came only later.

To get a feel for how Luther felt about Mary, read what he said in his Christmas sermon from 1531:

> [She is the] highest woman and the noblest gem in Christianity after Christ. . . . She is nobility, wisdom, and holiness personified. We can never honor her enough. Still honor and praise must be given to her in such a way as to injure neither Christ nor the Scriptures.

Which is, of course exactly what the Catholic Church has always taught, and continues to teach today.

SO WHAT YOU SAY IS . . .

❏ Catholic and Eastern Orthodox teachings about Mary are rooted in what the Bible says about Mary. It says she was "full of grace" — totally blessed by God.

❏ All of the Church's teachings about Mary have been embraced by Christians from ancient times. Even the first Protestant Reformer, Martin Luther, believed them.

❏ Catholics honor Mary because she played such an important role in bringing Jesus into the world. We don't worship Mary. We honor her as our mother in faith, and we ask her to pray for us.

TWELVE

"Why Does Your Church Have Statues?"

This is going to be serious. (You can tell because, right here and right now, the fundamentalist Christian in your life is making a pretty astonishing accusation: that Catholics live, breathe and worship in constant violation of one of the Ten Commandments.)

Why? Because, you see, the very first commandment says

You shall not carve idols for yourselves in the shape of anything in the sky above or on the earth below or in the waters beneath the earth; you shall not bow down before them or worship them. (EXODUS 20:4-5)

And so, you brave Catholic kid you, can you tell me exactly why there are statues of Jesus, Mary, Joseph, and who knows what saints in Catholic churches?

Why do Catholics even have the very same kind of images right in their homes, in their pockets, and on the dashboards of their cars?

Why do Catholics place flowers at the feet of statues of Mary and slips of paper with prayers on them in between Joseph's toes and carry images of Our Lady of Guadalupe around in processions?

Why?

Doesn't this seem to violate a law that God Himself laid down?

And you call yourself a Christian.

Right.

It's really okay.

Don't worry. You've figured out by now that if there wasn't an answer to this question, we wouldn't even be discussing it.

Let's begin the way we always do, and the way we always should: by looking at the context of the Bible passage being waved around in front of your very surprised face.

What is God telling the people of Israel here? What is He saying to His Chosen People, just freed from Egyptian slavery and oppression, about to endure a lot of suffering during forty years in the desert and all of the temptations that all of the pagan religions they'll meet along the way are going to offer?

He's obviously telling them to stay away from false gods and the idols that pagan religions constructed for their worship, many of which were represented by shapes of things that lived "in the sky above or on the earth below or in the waters beneath the earth."

Yup, that's pretty clear, isn't it?

That first commandment is all about idolatry and false gods, not about church artwork.

After all, if you *really* wanted to do a super-strict interpretation of the passage, you would take the Islamic approach. Muslims, whose holy book, the Koran, also includes the Ten Commandments, interpret this law as prohibiting any kind of artistic representation of anything in creation at all. That's why, when you look at Islamic buildings, you see that the decorations are all geometric — elaborate, intertwining shapes and lines, as well as gorgeous calligraphy.

It's clear that both Muslims and fundamentalist Christians are over-interpreting this passage. How do we know? By looking at the rest of the Bible and seeing what it has to say about using images in worship.

First of all, when you look at the Old Testament, you see cherubim — a kind of angel — all over the place. They're not only appearing to people, but — and this is the interesting part — images of them are being built in worship spaces.

By God's orders, by the way.

Take a look at Exodus 25:18-20 and 1 Chronicles 28:18-19. How could it be that what they say God's forbidding in one place, He's *commanding* in another?

Practicing What They Preach

It's clear, then, what the First Commandment is really all about: It's a prohibition of idolatry and construction of false idols, *not* images used as reminders of the one true God.

After all, you might wonder, does your friend have, anywhere in her possession, a poster or a drawing of Jesus? Might there be a print of Jesus or the Last Supper hanging in her parents' or grandparents' house? How about in her Sunday school classroom or in a Bible?

Wouldn't all of those be violations of the First Commandment, as she's interpreting it?

What Art Is All About

See, the difference between the Catholic and fundamentalist view is essentially this: Catholics aren't afraid of art.

(And neither, by the way, are the Eastern Orthodox. Episcopalians, Lutherans, and a lot of Presbyterians and Methodists aren't either — their churches may not have statues, but a lot of them have gorgeous stained glass windows featuring scenes from the life of Jesus.)

Art thaws even the frozen, darkened soul, opening it to lofty spiritual experiences. Through art, we are sometimes sent — indistinctly, briefly — revelations not to be achieved by rational thought.

ALEXANDER SOLZHENITSYN, *from his speech accepting the Nobel Prize for Literature*

We know, of course, that there's a risk that comes with art or any material thing we use to remind us of the holy. People can very easily slip into trouble from seeing the cross around their neck, the Bible in their backpack or the WWJD? bracelet around their wrist as good-luck charms or protective talismans, instead of as just good, simple reminders of God's presence and care.

It can happen with statues and other kinds of art, too. But the important thing your fundamentalist friend needs to understand is that the Catholic Church has always and forever stood very firmly against idolatry of any kind. Take a look at what the *Catechism of the Catholic Church* says about it:

> Idolatry is a perversion of man's innate religious sense. An idolater is someone who "transfers his indestructible notion of God to anything other than God." (No. 2114)

So it's perfectly clear to everyone now that the Catholic use of art in worship spaces isn't idolatrous — they are reminders to us of the holy, reminders that we creatures with the senses of sight and hearing and touch so sorely need. We don't worship them. We don't see them as having powers. They simply help us focus on God and the good He's done through His saints.

Most of us need all the help we can get, don't we?

SO WHAT YOU SAY IS . . .

❏ Catholics do not worship statues. We worship God. It doesn't matter what your friend's church has taught her about Catholic beliefs and practice. You find the truth about the Catholic Church by listening to what the Catholic Church says about itself, not what its opponents say.

❏ Catholics use art in churches as a way to remind us of God's presence, the same way photographs of relatives remind us of those we love.

❏ There's no difference between the Catholic use of art in churches and a fundamentalist Christian's use of an image of Jesus on a T-shirt, a poster, or a wall print.

THIRTEEN

"Why Do You Believe That the Pope Is Infallible?"

Actually, the questions about the pope that you're going to be fielding from your fundamentalist Christian friend won't be as sophisticated as this.

They'll be more like "So — why do Catholics have to do everything the pope says?" or "Why do you Catholics obey a man instead of God?" or "Why do Catholics think that the pope is perfect?"

And, as usual, you'll sit there wondering (a) where he came up with this stuff, (b) why fundamentalist Christian denominations teach lies about the Catholic Church, and (c) what, exactly, you're going to say next.

It's not as bad as you think. Let's get going.

Who's the Pope?

Let's deal with some definitions, first.

The pope is, quite simply, the successor to Peter, the apostle to whom Jesus said:

> *"And so I say to you, you are Peter, and upon this rock I will build my church, and the gates of the netherworld shall not prevail against it. I will give you the keys to the kingdom of heaven. Whatever you bind on earth shall be bound in heaven; and whatever you loose on earth shall be loosed in heaven."* (MATTHEW 16:18-19)

Can we get any clearer than that?

A quick tour through history makes it clear how we got from Peter to the present-day pope.

Jesus, of course, gave all of His apostles a very important responsibility: to continue His ministry of healing, teaching, and forgiveness. After being empowered by the Holy Spirit at Pentecost, that's exactly what the apostles did: They spread out through the Mediterranean area (even farther – historical tradition indicates that the apostle Thomas went all the way to India!), spreading the Good News about Jesus and starting Christian communities wherever they went.

The apostles were, it's obvious, the first leaders of the Christian Church. Because they had known Jesus personally and had been taught by Him, of course their authority was trusted and accepted — it's the beginning, as we mentioned several chapters ago, of Sacred Tradition.

The very early Christian communities weren't, of course, as consistently organized as churches are today. But surprisingly quickly, patterns of organization did evolve, centered on the roles of the *presbyter* (the precursor of what we call "priests" today), the leader of a local Christian community; the *diakonos* (obviously similar to today's deacons), whose ministry focused on ministry to the poor, the widows, and the orphans; and finally the *episkopos*. That Greek word *episkopos* literally means "overseer," and these men were indeed those whose ministry it was to oversee the Christian Church in an entire town or city. They were seen as the successors to the apostles, and today we call them "bishops."

By the way, this pattern of organization is described in Paul's First Letter to Timothy, Chapter 3. You might ask your "Bible-only" friend if his denomination has all of these leadership ministries; and if they don't, why not.

Anyway, rather quickly, certain cities became more important in the Christian world than others, mostly because of their size and their relation to the Roman Empire. The bishops of cities like Alexandria and Jerusalem were acknowledged as leaders among leaders. Most important of these cities, as you might guess, was Rome.

Rome wasn't just important because it was the capital of the Roman Empire, though. Christians valued Rome for another reason: It was where Peter spent the last part of his life, where he led the Christian community, and where, ultimately, he was martyred.

So, of course, historically speaking, it makes perfect sense that since Jesus Himself had named Peter the "rock" upon which He was going to build the Church and the one in possession of the "keys to the kingdom," the leadership of the Church in Rome would have a special role, a role we call "primacy."

There you have it — a thumbnail historical sketch of why the pope, or the bishop of Rome, is so important to Catholics:

- Jesus gave Peter special authority.
- Peter led the Christian Church in Rome.
- Just as Jesus passed on His authority to teach and lead to Peter, that authority was passed on to Peter's successors.

Once again, we've started with a question that seems to put Catholics on the spot, but which, upon reflection, really turns the spotlight on the fundamentalist Christian.

Jesus obviously gave Peter and the apostles special authority. So you can ask your fundamentalist friend, "What's your church's connection to Peter and the authority Jesus gave him?"

More Papal Matters

Sorry for the history lesson, but it was really necessary. You and your friend both need to understand that authority in the Catholic Church isn't arbitrary or dependent on human whim or on the votes of a congregation. It's ultimately rooted in Jesus' very clear directions to His apostles, and the responsibility, which He gave them.

So now, let's try to make some sense of this idea called "infallibility."

Let's start by saying what it is *not*:

- First of all, it's not something the pope "is." It's really not correct to say that "the pope is infallible." It's more accurate to talk about the pope "teaching infallibly." The idea doesn't describe the pope as a person; it describes a way in which God empowers him to teach.
- Secondly, saying that the pope can teach infallibly doesn't mean that the pope is sinless. Popes go to confession, just like every other Catholic.
- It doesn't mean that everything the pope says about any subject is correct. The definition of infallibility is actually really narrow. It doesn't cover the pope's ability to do math problems, predict the weather, or give his view of political issues. It doesn't even cover every single religious issue.

So what is infallibility all about?

Infallibility is about faith. It's about the basics of faith, the nuts and bolts, all the stuff that God has given to us through His revelation. It's about Jesus keeping His promise to be with us until the end of time, His promise that the Holy Spirit would always be with the Church, no matter what.

To put it really simply, it's about protection.

Through the gift of infallibility, God ensures that the leaders of the Church will teach the truth of faith (including teachings about morals) without error. It might surprise you to know that infallibility isn't just a gift given to the pope; it's a gift given to the bishops as a group (in union with the pope), and one which is exercised by the pope in a special way, since he's the head of the bishops and is Peter's successor.

So no, popes, bishops, and Church councils don't go running around issuing "infallible" statements all the time. Since so much of the Church's teaching has been assumed to be authoritative and true — like what's in the Nicene and Apostles' Creeds, if you want to get specific — the only time it is necessary to teach infallibly is when a question arises, or when a heresy (a belief that presents itself as Christian, but really isn't) is threatening to tear the Church apart.

Do you get it? Infallibility is basically the gift God gives the Church to ensure that the fundamentals of faith and morals, as revealed by Him through Scripture and Tradition, is maintained and passed on unchanged.

If you think about this, it makes perfect sense, really, and it does one other thing that's very important: It takes the words of Jesus in the Gospels very, very seriously.

Didn't Jesus say that He would be with the Church until the end of time?

Didn't Jesus give the apostles the responsibility to teach in His name?

Didn't Jesus promise the "Spirit of Truth" to the Church? (John 14:17)

If all that's true, then it's obvious that what we call "The Church" is something a lot more solid than just a bunch of people who get together to sing and listen to preaching.

Obviously, Jesus intended for it to be more than that. He intended for the leaders of the Church to pass on the Good News of God's love in concrete, clear ways that were — and here's the rub — trustworthy.

The whole idea of infallibility is about no more or less than that. Jesus said He would be with the Church until the end of time. Catholics happen to believe Him. Because of Jesus' promises, we're confident that the faith we're taught is true.

Don't you wonder where the fundamentalist's confidence comes from? Does it come from his pastor's interpretation of the Bible, which of course differs a lot from the interpretation of the Bible preached by the pastor of another church right down the street?

Isn't it great to have a confidence that's rooted in God's Word instead of the words of human beings?

Isn't it?

SO WHAT YOU SAY IS . . .

❏ History traces the Catholic papacy back to the apostle Peter, who received his authority to lead the Church from Jesus Himself.

❏ From ancient times, Christians have believed that the bishop of Rome (the pope) had a special role to play in the Church — not because of any personal powers, but because of the authority Jesus gave him.

❏ Infallibility is a gift from Jesus to the Church. It's the grace in which God protects the Church from teaching error in matters of faith and morals. Since bishops are the heirs to the apostles, and are the primary teachers in our Church, the gift of infallibility rests with them as a group (united with the pope), and with the pope as the most important of the bishops.

❑ Infallibility is rooted in Jesus' promise that He would be with the Church always, until the end of time.

FOURTEEN

"Why Do You Confess to a Priest?"

This is a good one.

It's good because the answer is so simple, and even better, it's totally biblically-based, so clear and obvious that you can't help but wonder how your "Bible-only" fundamentalist friend is going to cope.

When you get the confession question, get out your Bible. Open it to the Gospel of John, Chapter 20, and point to verses 19-23. Invite your friend to read out loud. We'll pick it up at verse 21:

> [Jesus] said to them again, "Peace be with you. As the Father has sent me, so I send you." And when he had said this, he breathed on them and said to them, "Receive the holy Spirit. Whose sins you forgive are forgiven them, and whose sins you retain are retained."

There. Next question?

Okay, I guess we can give it a little more explanation, although the implications — no, the plain, literal meaning — of this text is really perfectly clear. It all goes back to our sense of what the Church is, a sense which is, of course, quite firmly rooted in Scripture.

Jesus came to earth to bring salvation to the world. He did this by preaching, teaching and healing, living, dying, and rising from the dead. All of these acts were directed toward one purpose: to bring people into relationship with God, into the forgiving arms of the Father.

He selected a bunch of guys to help Him — the apostles. Over and over throughout the Gospels, we see Jesus empowering these apostles, sending them out, and directing them to act in His name.

That's the Church, right? It's the presence of Jesus on earth — that's why we, taking our cue from St. Paul, call the Church the "Body of Christ." The Church continues Jesus' work on earth, just as He wanted it to.

A major part of that work, of course, is the forgiveness of sins.

Now, completely ignoring the passage you just read together, your friend is going to object, saying that only God forgives sins. Why do Catholics think that God's forgiveness has to come through a priest?

Well, Catholics *don't*, in fact, say that all of God's forgiveness "has to" come through one of the Church's ordained ministers. If that were true, we wouldn't ever say

the Act of Contrition on our own — but we do. If that were so, we wouldn't ever be encouraged to perform a daily examination of conscience, asking God's forgiveness for the sins we've committed that day — but we do.

And if that were so, every single Catholic Mass wouldn't include a rite of penance in which we, as a community gathered in the liturgy, ask God's forgiveness for sins either through a litany ("Lord have mercy . . .") or through the *Confiteor* ("I confess to almighty God . . .").

Be sure to point out these realities of Catholic life to your friend. Penitential prayer for both individuals and our community is a vital, basic part of Catholic spirituality.

But what about those words of Jesus?

Here's the deal. We take them seriously.

For it's absolutely true, as the *Catechism of the Catholic Church* says, "Only God forgives sins" (no. 1441). But how is that forgiveness mediated — or given — to us?

Explain it to your friend this way.

God is love, right? God's love is ever-present, overflowing, rich, and abundant. But do any of us, aside from the most profound mystics and saints, walk around in total awareness of God's love for us all the time?

I doubt it. I also doubt that every single experience of God's love has come to you or your friend in the complete solitude of prayer, moments "just between" you and God.

I'll bet that you've experience God's love, most of all, through other people: your parents and other relatives, your friends and the sense of care and community you experience in a youth group or worship service.

I'll bet there are even moments in life when you've actually *forgotten* what God's love is all about, have reached a point in which you don't think you'll ever be able to really feel it again, but are suddenly lifted up by some kind of reminder from another human being that, hey, you're a lovable and deeply loved child of God.

Do you see?

The love of God was always there, but because of our human limitations, it has to be mediated. God doesn't mind sharing His love for us through other people. In fact, it might even be part of the point of creation, right?

It's the exact same thing with God's forgiveness. Yes, God is the forgiver of sins. But how does that forgiveness come to us?

Jesus indicates, in that passage from John, that He wants it to come to us through those He's sent to minister in His name.

When you look at it that way, this sacrament we call the "Sacrament of Reconciliation" isn't a burden or a law — it's a beautiful, astonishing gift from Jesus Himself.

Jesus knows how hard the road to forgiveness and healing is.

He knows how our hearts can so easily be taken over with doubts about God's forgiveness.

He knows what kind of strength we can get from the authoritative assurance that "Yes, your sins are forgiven."

So He gave us this sacrament, as John 20:23 makes very clear.

You should be seeing a pattern, one that's been continuing throughout this book. The fundamentalist Christian likes to criticize Catholics for having a lot of stuff that's "man-made" — sacraments, authority, Sacred Tradition, and so on.

Isn't it clear by now that all of that is rooted, not in human actions or will, but in the will of Christ for His people?

Jesus established the Christian community to be His Body on earth, to continue His ministry. That Body doesn't act out of it's own authority, but out of the authority of Christ Himself, and out of His presence with us, as passages like this one make very clear. As the *Catechism* says, in relation to this sacrament in particular, "The confessor is not the master of God's forgiveness, but its servant" (no. 1466).

And one could say that about every aspect of the Church: It exists to serve God by spreading His Word and doing His work, and it exists to serve the world by announcing the Good News of love, forgiveness, and healing.

So the answer to this one is pretty simple, isn't it?

Catholics are reconciled to God in a lot of ways, but of great importance to us is the Sacrament of Reconciliation, in which we hear the words of God's forgiveness loud and clear.

Why is it so important?

Because Jesus gave it to us, that's why.

SO WHAT YOU SAY IS . . .

❑ Catholics believe that forgiveness for sins comes from God.

❑ God shares this forgiveness with us in many ways. Included in this is the Sacrament of Reconciliation.

❑ Catholics believe that God works through this sacrament to forgive sins because Jesus said He does in the Gospel of John.

FIFTEEN

"Why Do You Call Priests 'Father'?"

For some reason, fundamentalist Christians think that is little area of discussion practically closes the book on Catholicism. It's strange, I know, but it's true: The fact that we call our priests "father" pretty much puts the nail in the coffin of our purported fidelity to Christ — in their eyes, at least.

It all comes down to one little verse in Scripture — Matthew 23:9. In this passage, Jesus is preaching, it's said, "to the crowds and to his disciples." He's talking about leadership, specifically about how the scribes and Pharisees don't practice what they preach. He condemns them, in particular, for seeking worldly honor and prestige. In this context, Jesus says to His disciples:

> *"As for you, do not be called, 'Rabbi.' You have but one teacher, and you are all brothers. Call no one on earth your father; you have but one Father in heaven. Do not be called 'Master'; you have but one master, the Messiah. The greatest among you must be your servant."*
> (MATTHEW 23:8-11)

It's pretty clear what Jesus is warning against, isn't it? He's warning His disciples to remember who they are and are not: They are not God. They are servants, called to teach and preach God's Word; but they are most definitely not God, and they need to remember that.

He doesn't exactly seem to be laying down rules for forms of address, does He?

Well, sorry, but to the fundamentalist Christian, that's exactly what Jesus is doing there, and because, Miss (or Mr.) Catholic, your Church doesn't have a problem with priests being called "Father," that very same Church is obviously in direct violation of Jesus' words.

So how can you call yourself a Christian?

I'm sure that by now this practice of taking Bible verses completely and totally out of context is beginning to drive you a little bit nuts. But at least you know what to expect, right?

There are a couple of angles from which to tackle this problem — which isn't, of course, really a problem at all.

The first thing is to ask if your friend ever refers to his dad as his "father."

If he does — uh-oh.

Isn't he disobeying Jesus if he does?

No? Why not?

Your friend will undoubtedly say that Jesus wasn't talking about family relations here, that He was talking about how to refer to religious leaders.

There are a couple of minor points you are perfectly welcome to raise here.

First, how does your friend know exactly who and what Jesus was talking about? How do they know He wasn't talking about family relations? It's not explicitly stated, so it seems as if there's a bit of (gasp!) interpretation going on here, isn't there? We thought that was against the biblical-literalist rules.

Secondly — and this is minor, but instructive neverthe-less — does your friend really think that in the middle of this rather profound, important passage about humility and service, Jesus would stop to offer a list of forbidden personal titles?

I mean, if He were going to do that, why didn't He go ahead and include "Reverend" — a very common title for Protestant ministers, by the way — which is rooted in a word meaning "honored for being holy?" Wouldn't that have been more to the point?

After you've brought up enough questions about the legitimacy of your friend's general approach to this passage, let's look at the specifics. Specifically, let's look at the rest of the New Testament and check out if Paul and other early Christian leaders took Jesus' words "literally."

Well, even if they took the "father" stuff at its "plain, literal meaning," they sure ignored the first part of the passage, in which, your fundamentalist friend must admit, Jesus seems to be forbidding the use of the title *teacher*, which is what *rabbi* means. Paul used the term quite a lot in his letters. Take a look at Ephesians 4:11 and 1 Corinthians 12:28.

Do you know what else? Do you know what's even more amazing than the use of the title *teacher*? Paul constantly — and I mean *constantly* — uses the father-child analogy as a way to describe his relationship with his own co-workers:

> To Timothy, my true child in faith: grace, mercy, and peace from God the Father and Christ Jesus our Lord. (1 TIMOTHY 1:2)

> But you know his worth, how as a child with a father he served along with me in the cause of the gospel. (PHILIPPIANS 2:22)

And then there's this one, addressed to the Christian community in Corinth:

> Even if you should have countless guides to Christ, yet you do not have many fathers, for I became your father in Christ Jesus through the gospel. (1 CORINTHIANS 4:15)

It's a simple question, really. What does your fundamentalist friend make of all of these references? How can he say that Jesus was laying down a strict rule of address when Paul apparently didn't see it that way?

It's clear now — isn't it? — that Jesus *wasn't* laying down rules of address in that passage. (How out of character that would have been for Jesus, anyway!) No, Jesus was speaking to His disciples, in particular, about the humility necessary for religious leaders. He was warning them to remember that God is the ultimate Teacher, the supreme Father, and the one Master. Whenever they were tempted to behave as the scribes and Pharisees were doing, they needed to step back and remember that very important reality.

One More Thing

If your friend is determined to interpret this passage as a concrete directive, why don't you run through some other rather concrete directives laid down in the New Testament and ask if he or his church congregation obeys every one of them to the letter, like this one:

> When you pray, go to your inner room, close the door, and pray to your Father in secret. (MATTHEW 6:6)

Does his congregation have public worship services? Why? Doesn't Jesus forbid them here?

And then there are these:

> If anyone comes to me without hating his father and mother, wife and children, brothers and sisters, and even his own life, he cannot be my disciple. (LUKE 14:26)

> Any woman who prays or prophesies with her head unveiled brings shame upon her head. (1 CORINTHIANS 11:5)

I sincerely doubt that your friend or his congregation determines anyone's Christianity — including their own — by how these passages are lived out. He'll say, with complete justification, that you have to interpret these passages, that Jesus was speaking metaphorically — or that, in the last, Paul was speaking to people of a particular culture.

Fine, good and dandy. Great.

But then why decide, out of all of these passages (and many more we could name) that Matthew 23:9 must be viewed "literally" but, as we've seen, completely out of context as some sort of rule of address that all true Christians must obey?

He won't say it, but I will.

Because it's something Catholics do, that's why. And that's the only reason. Period.

SO WHAT YOU SAY IS . . .

❏ The titles that Catholics give their leaders are like those of any other religious tradition: They evolved over time as an expression of what those symbols symbolize to us.

❏ The idea of spiritual leaders being like fathers to children is an ancient one, and is expressed many times in the New Testament.

❏ To take Jesus' words in Matthew 23:9 as a rule about forms of address is to take His words wildly out of context. If one insists on interpreting it literally, one must admit that even Paul himself violated it time and time again.

SIXTEEN

"Why Do You Believe in Purgatory?"

When you're discussing purgatory — this oddest of Catholic teachings to the fundamentalist — it's important to make some important things very clear right away:

- Purgatory is not a "place." It's not a "middle region" between heaven and hell.
- Purgatory isn't a sort of low-grade spot for folks who didn't sin badly enough to merit the eternally painful fires of hell.
- Catholics don't pay to "get out" of purgatory. Catholics don't do things to "earn" days off from purgatory.

Your fundamentalist Christian friend isn't going to believe you. She's going to insist that Catholics really do believe all those things. All you can do in response is tell her, over and over, that we don't, and point out to her the three paragraphs of the *Catechism of the Catholic Church* that deal with purgatory, one of which reads simply this way:

> All who die in God's grace and friendship, but still imperfectly purified, are indeed assured of their eternal salvation; but after death they undergo purification, so as to achieve the holiness necessary to enter the joy of heaven. (No. 1030).

If you keep reading the *Catechism*, you'll see that nowhere does it describe this process in detail, and nowhere does it say a single word about days or money or even fire.

She has to understand that it doesn't matter what her pastor said about purgatory. It doesn't matter what the anti-Catholic pamphlet she read said about it either. Getting reliable information about Catholic beliefs from sources like those is just about as likely as getting an accurate history of the United States from an old Communist Russian textbook.

It's just not going to happen.

The best thing to do in a situation like that is to simply persist. Very rationally describe exactly what the Catholic Church really and truly teaches about purgatory, which we've already done, then go ahead and do the next thing we're about to do: Talk about how much sense the teaching makes, and how it's supported by — believe it or not — the Bible.

The Afterlife: A Mystery

The things we say about purgatory have something in common with anything we say about the afterlife: We can only go so far.

Sure, our imaginations take us further — either into a heaven with an ideal, gorgeous landscape, or a hell filled with devilish imps torturing the damned with pitchforks. But the truth is, we really don't know much.

All we can really say for sure about either is what's been revealed to us:

- In heaven, our sanctified immortal souls live in perfect joy with God in eternity.
- In hell, souls, by their own free choice, are separated from communion with God forever.

Heaven and hell are very real — Jesus speaks of them both, of course — but it's not quite accurate to insist on speaking of them as physical "places." When we're talking about God, we're talking about the realm of the spirit, of eternity, of existence outside the created boundaries of time and space. So the plain fact is, after death, there is no such thing as time, and there is no such thing as space — those are both a part of created reality.

So be careful when you talk about these things. Make sure you're not talking on a second-grade, Sunday school level about the afterlife; but also make clear that to say that the afterlife is essentially about "states of being" rather than physical time and space *is not* saying that heaven and hell are "states of mind" or anything less than very, very real. They are real — they're just beyond the reality that we can grasp while we're still on earth.

So it goes with purgatory. It's not a place — as the *Catechism* explains, it's really a process. It's a process of purification. Quite simply, since nothing impure or blemished with sin can live in God's presence, and hardly any of us die with perfectly reconciled souls, it makes sense for God to give us a chance to set that right after death. It makes sense for God to continue to shower His healing graces on us, even after our physical lives have ended.

"Okay, okay," your friend says, probably bored out her mind right now with your musings on the afterlife. "But *why* do Catholics believe this? It's not in the Bible, after all."

It's not? Oh really?

Perhaps the word "purgatory" isn't in the Bible, but there are some odd little statements scattered here and there throughout Scripture that give us hints of the truth of this teaching.

Paul says that if, after death, a person's life is found wanting, *that one will suffer loss; the person will be saved, but only as through fire."* (1 Corinthians 3:15)

This is an interesting passage, because it implies that after death, a person whose soul isn't perfectly clean and worthy to live forever in the presence of God still has a chance to be saved, but only through some kind of painful process.

Would this kind of painful process exist in heaven? Of course not — our souls don't endure pain in heaven. So what could Paul be talking about?

Perhaps he's talking about the chance for purification that does indeed come after death, the process we today call "purgatory."

And then, in the Old Testament, we find this passage, which, in reference to praying for the dead, says:

It was a holy and pious thought. Thus he made atonement for the dead that they might be freed from this sin. ·
(2 Maccabees 12:45-46)

Do souls in heaven bear sin? Do they need prayer? No.

Do souls in hell, there by their own choice for eternity, benefit from prayer? No.

If there's only heaven and hell, what purpose would praying for the dead serve? None at all. But it's mentioned, and it's mentioned approvingly, so that tells us, once again, that God's mercy doesn't end with physical death.

Now, your friend, is going to point out, and quickly too, that the Old Testament passage you mentioned up there was from one of the books that Protestants don't accept. True. But here's what you can say in response:

"You're right. But as we talked about before, that book of Maccabees *was* accepted by all Christians as God's Word for fifteen hundred years before the Reformation. In fact, the only real reason that Martin Luther decided that book had to go was because of that particular passage, which supported the teaching on purgatory, a teaching he rejected.

"Does that really seem right to you?"

Here we have a teaching believed by all Christians for hundreds of years, supported by Scripture that was accepted by Christians for hundreds of years. Along comes one guy who decides that that teaching is wrong, then, on his own, decides that the book of the Bible that supports it doesn't belong in the Bible anymore. What a coincidence!

What a strange way to form one's beliefs: based on the opinions of one guy, rather than the consistent witness of the Church.

That's About It

You're probably not going to be able to make much more progress on this purgatory business. But if you've gotten this far with your friend, you've done really well. You've helped her understand that our belief in purgatory is rooted in a profound respect for God's glory, as well as in hints scattered throughout Scripture that indicate that God has the power, the will, and the desire to continue to offer us forgiveness even after death.

It's also interesting to mention that one of the most famous and revered Protestant Christians of the twentieth century happened to believe in purgatory. His name was C.S. Lewis, and in his *Letters to Malcolm*, he said:

> Of course I pray for the dead. . . . I believe in Purgatory. . . . Our souls *demand* Purgatory, don't they?

SO WHAT YOU SAY IS . . .

❑ Purgatory is the stage after death in which our souls undergo a final sanctification, so that we'll be pure and worthy to be in God's presence, which is what heaven is.

❑ There are hints of purgatory in Scripture, both in the Old and New Testaments.

❑ Purgatory has been a part of Christian belief for most of Christian history, and has even been accepted by some Protestants.

EPILOGUE

It's All About Love

I certainly hope your friendship has survived all of this intense discussion.

If it has, congratulations!

That means you've conducted yourself in exactly the right way: rationally, calmly, patiently — and, above all, with love.

For your goal in all of this hasn't been to win arguments for the sake of your own ego, right?

It's been to share the truth, which is a very loving thing to do.

You've probably noticed that every discussion in this book centers around that contentious matter we call "truth."

It's kind of unfashionable to think about truth, isn't it?

After all, most of the voices around you tell you that truth is completely relative (which is a contradiction in terms, of course), and that all religions are basically the same.

You've discovered that they're not.

It's very clear to you now that there are huge differences between fundamentalist Christianity and Catholicism. Before you started this discussion, you might have even been tempted to say that those differences were minor or irrelevant.

But no more, right?

We're not saying that good, holy people aren't a part of every religion on the planet. We're not saying that there aren't elements of truth in every religion.

What we are saying, though, is that when you look at the Bible and you look at history, it's pretty clear which church has the most direct line to Christ. It's also clear which church takes the whole of God's revelation seriously, rather than just a part.

That's not to say that there haven't been times in which elements of the Catholic Church have strayed. The Church may have been called into existence by Jesus Christ, but it is a human institution nonetheless. Members of the Church sin. Sometimes even Church teachers misunderstand God's Word or emphasize the wrong parts of it. Sometimes the whole Church has to be shaken into closer fidelity to Christ by visionary voices like St. Francis of Assisi, St. Catherine of Siena — or even by challengers like Martin Luther.

But through it all, the lines of connection have never been broken between the life of Christ in the Church today and the life of Christ on earth two thousand years ago. Your reading of this book should make this obvious: God's Word remains mysterious, and must be constantly clarified for each new generation. But even given those limitations, you can see that every central doctrine and practice of the Catholic Church can be traced back to Jesus and the apostles. All the way back.

So, yes, this is all about love.

It's a loving act to share the truth about Jesus.

It's a loving act to encourage honesty in faith.

It's even loving to point out difficult and incomplete elements of other faiths.

As long as, of course, we ourselves remain humble.

As long as we remember that as close as our Church's teaching and sacramental life bring us to Christ, we still, like Paul, "see indistinctly, as in a mirror" (1 Corinthians 13:12), while we live on this earth.

We wait for the day when we, and all those we love, will see the Truth as He is:

> *For we know partially and we prophesy partially, but when the perfect comes, the partial will pass away. . . . At present I know partially; then I shall know fully, as I am fully known.* (1 CORINTHIANS 13: 9-10, 12)

FOR A DEEPER LOOK

Books

Born Fundamentalist, Born Again Catholic by David Currie (Ignatius Press)

By What Authority?: An Evangelical Discovers Catholic Tradition by Mark P. Shea (Our Sunday Visitor)

Catholic and Christian: An Explanation of Commonly Misunderstood Catholic Beliefs by Alan Schreck (Servant Publications)

The Catholic Church and the Bible by Father Peter M.J. Stravinksas (Ignatius Press)

Catholicism and Fundamentalism: The Attack on 'Romanism' by 'Bible Christians' by Karl Keating (Ignatius Press)

The How-To Book of Catholic Devotions by Mike Aquilina and Regis J. Flaherty (Our Sunday Visitor)

Surprised by Truth: 11 Converts Give the Biblical and Historical Reasons for Becoming Catholic edited by Patrick Madrid (Basilica Press)

What Catholics Really Believe: 52 Answers to Common Misconceptions About the Faith by Karl Keating (Ignatius Press)

Where is That in the Bible? by Patrick Madrid (Our Sunday Visitor)

Why Do Catholics Do That?: A Guide to the Teachings and Practices of the Catholic Church by Kevin Orlin Johnson (Ballantine Books)

Websites

Biblical Evidence for Catholicism **http://ic.net/~erasmus**

Catholic Answers **http://www.catholicanswers.com**

Nazareth Resource Library **http://www.cin.org/users/james/index.htm**

ABOUT THE AUTHOR

Amy Welborn has a master's degree in religion from Vanderbilt University. She taught high school theology for nine years before devoting all of her time to writing. Since 1994, she has been writing a syndicated column on Catholic youth for Catholic News Service and is a regular columnist in *Our Sunday Visitor*. She is the author of the book *Prove It! God* (Our Sunday Visitor).

God, the first in the **Prove It!** series, answers the *real* questions you have about God, the Catholic Church, other religions, evolution, good and evil, and a whole lot of other things you never hear about in religion classes, Sunday sermons, or from your parents. But don't take our word for it. Read **Prove It! God** and decide for yourself. What do you have to lose besides your doubts?

PROVE IT! GOD
By Amy Welborn
0-87973-396-9 (396), paper, 128 pp.

Available at bookstores. MasterCard, VISA, and Discover customers can order direct from **Our Sunday Visitor** by calling **1-800-348-2440**. Order online at www.osv.com.

Our Sunday Visitor
200 Noll Plaza
Huntington, IN 46750
1-800-348-2440
e-mail: osvbooks@osv.com

Availability of books subject to change without notice.

Our Sunday Visitor . . .
Your Source for Discovering
the Riches of the Catholic Faith

Our Sunday Visitor has an extensive line of materials for young children, teens, and adults. Our books, Bibles, booklets, CD-ROMs, audios, and videos are available in bookstores worldwide.

To receive a FREE full-line catalog or for more information, call **Our Sunday Visitor** at **1-800-348-2440**. Or write, **Our Sunday Visitor** / 200 Noll Plaza / Huntington, IN 46750.

- -

Please send me: ___A catalog
Please send me materials on:

___Apologetics and catechetics   ___Reference works
___Prayer books   ___Heritage and the saints
___The family   ___The parish

Name_____
Address_____Apt._____
City_____State____Zip_____
Telephone (   ) _____

A19BBABP

- -

Please send a friend: ___A catalog
Please send a friend materials on:

____Apologetics and catechetics   ____Reference works
____Prayer books   ____Heritage and the saints
____The family   ____The parish

Name_____
Address_____Apt._____
City_____State____Zip_____
Telephone (   ) _____

A19BBABP

- -

Our Sunday Visitor
200 Noll Plaza
Huntington, IN 46750
Toll free: **1-800-348-2440**
E-mail: osvbooks@osv.com
Website: www.osv.com